Zotero

A GUIDE FOR LIBRARIANS, RESEARCHERS AND EDUCATORS

by Jason Puckett

D1249210

Association of College and Research Libraries
A division of the American Library Association
Chicago, Illinois 2011

The paper used in this publication meets the minimum requirements of American National Standard for Information Sciences–Permanence of Paper for Printed Library Materials, ANSI Z39.48-1992. ∞

Library of Congress Cataloging-in-Publication Data

Puckett, Jason, 1969-
  Zotero : a guide for librarians, researchers, and educators / by Jason Puckett.
       p. cm.
  Includes bibliographical references.
  ISBN 978-0-8389-8589-2 (pbk. : alk. paper) 1. Zotero. 2. Bibliographical citations--Computer programs. 3. Citation of electronic information resources--Computer programs. I. Title.
  PN171.F56P83 2011
  025.30285'536--dc23
                        2011017430

Printed in the United States of America.

15 14 13 12 11   5 4 3 2 1

The cover design by Christian Steinmetz includes the following Creative Commons-licensed images:
"DVD Cover" by Patrick Emerson: flickr.com/photos/kansasphoto/5342478807
"mire, mire qué locura!..." by Gisela Giardino: flickr.com/photos/gi/168406150
"Free Texture #152" by Brenda Clarke: flickr.com/photos/brenda-starr/4684748856
"Interesting Things In My Library" by Rupert Scammell: flickr.com/photos/aus-sierupe/4242118524
"Soviet printed stationery 1962" by Felix O: flickr.com/photos/sludgeulper/3230949637

Table of Contents

Acknowledgments

I owe thanks to a great many people for their practical assistance, advice and moral support while I wrote this book. Among them are:

My editor Kathryn Deiss at ACRL for remaining unflaggingly patient, helpful and encouraging with this novice author.

Christian Steinmetz for designing the cover. I have some regrets over rejecting his original "robot superhero wielding a sword" design idea, but I was afraid it would promise a more exciting book than I could deliver.

Serge Clermont for suggesting the idea of using personas to provide real-world context for all these features, or as he put it "A day in the life of Zotero."

Erin Mooney, Zotero instructor extraordinaire at Emory University Library, Debbie Maron, CHNM's campus outreach guru, Zotero developer Faolan Cheslack-Postava, and Zotero director Sean Takats for being kind enough to read chapters in progress and provide me with feedback based on their own prodigious Zotero expertise.

All of the librarians, teachers and professors who took the time to share information about how they're using Zotero in class. I selected material from several of them to quote or cite in chapter 6 based mostly on my desire to include a representative variety, but several others not cited by name sent me material that informed both that chapter and the rest of the book, and I'm grateful to you all for your contributions.

As with anything I try to accomplish, my wife Anne Graham and my parents David and Priscilla Puckett never ceased to encourage me. Thank you all for believing I could do it.

Introduction

A few years ago I was working as a reference and instruction para-professional in an academic library. Among other things, I was the library's EndNote instructor and was (and am) a great fan of citation management software. In the evenings I was taking online graduate classes in library science, so I was also a student actively writing papers on a regular basis.

I had been regularly using EndNote, but had a laptop running the Linux operating system, which is incompatible with EndNote. I had been hearing about Zotero (zotero.org) for a few months, and installed it to try out since it worked with Linux and the OpenOffice word processor.

I was startled at how much easier it was to use than EndNote, and it quickly became my citation manager of choice. I began putting Zotero workshops on the library schedule alongside the EndNote ones, and found that students picked up the essentials of Zotero much faster and seemed more confident using it.

I use Zotero in my personal research, to save and organize sources for current and future projects, and to create bibliographies in any of the three word processors I use regularly. I use it to keep track of interesting books I want to read eventually (I have a Zotero collection of titles instead of a stack of books on my nightstand). I keep my Zotero library simultaneously on my Windows desktop at work, my Linux netbook at home, and online at the Zotero website. I'm using it as I write this book. I'm really not sure how I coped without it.

I've been a Zotero "evangelist" at two different libraries now, and it's extraordinarily rare that I encounter a student or professor who doesn't like it. I regularly incorporate a Zotero section into my information literacy class sessions, and I find I can teach the essentials in just a few minutes if that's all the time I have available. I also teach in-person and online workshops, and I get requests to give Zotero classes for courses from first-year composition to PhD seminars.

Several times a week I get Zotero support questions by email, instant message or via drop-in referrals at the reference desk. These are usually basic requests for a quick walkthrough of installing Zotero and saving citations, but can be almost anything. I have been called on to help professors set up shared libraries for their research assistants, troubleshoot odd technical problems, and on occasion explain what a web browser is to truly novice researchers.

How to Use this Book

Reference and instruction librarians like myself concern ourselves with library users' "information needs." Much of our professional activity is centered around determining what information a researcher requires (not always as easy as it sounds!) and connecting them with that information in a form they can use. I've thought a lot about the information needs of my potential readers as I planned this book.

Naturally I hope that everyone who picks up the book will read it through, but I've written it with a few different audiences in mind: researchers who just need a how-to guide to help them make bibliographies, instruction librarians and teachers using Zotero in conjunction with classes doing research assignments, and reference librarians and tech support staff who are helping users with Zotero questions and problems.

If you're "just" a researcher using Zotero, you should read chapter 1 if you have no idea what Zotero is for, but would probably be fine skipping ahead to chapter 2. The essentials for beginning users are in chapters 2 through 4. Definitely take a look at the information about synchronizing in chapter 5; it's handy for automatically backing up your library and accessing it easily from multiple computers.

If you're teaching Zotero workshops or providing Zotero support for a library or IT department, read the whole book. Chapters 6 and 7, about teaching and supporting Zotero, might be particularly useful.

If you're a librarian or educator using Zotero as a research tool in your academic classes, read the whole book with particular attention to the discussion of teaching in chapter 6. Chapter 7 may have some useful ideas for you.

What this Book *Doesn't* Cover

This book is written for users and teachers of Zotero, not developers or systems librarians. I won't be covering what I loosely think of as "programmer stuff." (That phrase should give you an idea of my qualifications as a programmer, i.e. none.)

To be a little more specific and less tongue-in-cheek, this book doesn't include topics like:

- writing site translators to allow Zotero to interpret metadata from your website
- creating Zotero plugins
- making your website compatible with Zotero by adding metadata

If you're interested in these topics and related ones, I'll refer you to the Zotero developer documentation at zotero.org/support/dev/start, and to the Zotero forums at forums.zotero.org.

My System

Zotero was designed to run on any operating system that will run the Firefox web browser (and now with Chrome and Safari, with a version for Internet Explorer coming soon). Its word processor plugins work with Microsoft Word, OpenOffice and NeoOffice. Most of what I cover is OS-agnostic: it will work the same way no matter what kind of computer you're using. However, I'm making an assumption up front that most people will be using Zotero for Firefox in the Windows OS, with Word 2007 as their word processor of choice. Unless I specify otherwise, you can usually safely assume that that's the setup I'm describing.

Fortunately, Zotero usually behaves consistently between different operating systems and even word processors: I have no trouble shifting mental gears and sharing files between Windows/Word at work and Linux/OpenOffice at home. I'm aware (for example) that MacOS may require a control-click instead of a right-click to bring up a context menu, but it's awkward to write "right-click or control-click" in every such case, so when it makes a difference I'm going with Windows. MacOS and Linux users are probably used to that assumption anyway.

At press time, I was using the following software for writing and testing:

- Zotero 2.1, the most recent version
- Windows XP on my office computer and Ubuntu Linux on my home netbook
- OpenOffice/Word 2007/Google docs
- Firefox version 4.0
- The alpha/test version of Standalone Zotero

I don't use MacOS myself, but whenever possible I imposed on Mac-Zotero-using friends to double-check my work and make sure I wasn't making any errors. Any mistakes that remain are my fault, not theirs.

At press time, Standalone Zotero—the version that works with Safari and Chrome—was in "alpha" stage, an early test version. I made the choice to be slightly less specific about the details of installing Standalone, since the alpha version is a bit rough and I expect you to be using a more sophisticated installer than the one I did.

The Word "Library"

I use "library" with two meanings in this book. The first sense you're familiar with: the big building with all the books that constitutes the heart and soul of the university campus, and provides students and faculty with all the databases, research tools, information literacy teaching, and excellent support and service they need for their research. (Yes, I'm proud to be a librarian.)

The second sense may be new to you if you haven't used reference manager software before. When you save a reference (like a book or article citation) using a program like Zotero, it goes into your personal collection of information on your hard drive or on the web. Most reference managers, including Zotero, call this your "library." This is the kind of library I'll be discussing most of the time, obviously. I think the distinction should be clear from context when I refer to the other kind.

Changes Happen

Any book about software inevitably starts to show its age even before it makes it to the shelf. Zotero changes and improves frequently: that's one of the things I appreciate about it. Depending on when you read this book there will no doubt be new Zotero versions with new features not covered here. I still expect this guide to remain useful for some time to come, however.

My experience with Zotero for the last several years indicates that their development path has stabilized along the lines of adding new features, but not making major changes to existing ones. That is, Zotero 2.0 introduced new features (syncing, group libraries and so on) that added new capabilities, but the basic save citation/create bibliography functions work almost exactly the same and wouldn't baffle a Zotero 1.0 user. (In contrast with, say, the struggle we all had adjusting from Word 2003 to 2007.) As far as I know, from my vantage point as an educator who talks to the Zotero developers from time to time, that's the road map for projected versions. In other words, I expect that this will still be a useful guide for the features that I do cover here even as new ones appear over time.

Also, this isn't just a software how-to manual, though the first part of the book is mostly that. I'll also be discussing my (and others') experience, recommendations and best practices for teaching and supporting Zotero. I expect and hope that that material will all remain relevant for years yet.

Finally, I maintain a Zotero guide for Georgia State University Library at research.library.gsu.edu/zotero. I keep it as up-to-date as I possibly can when new features are released, and post answers to our most frequently asked Zotero questions. The guide is licensed under Creative Commons, so you may also copy it and adapt it for your own institution as long as you credit me and GSU Library.

The name Zotero comes from an Albanian verb, *zotëroj*, meaning to master or acquire a skill. I hope this book will be a useful means for you to master whatever level of Zotero expertise you need.

CHAPTER 1 **About Zotero**

Let's start with the most basic question.

What's Zotero?

Zotero is a reference manager program. It exists either as an add-on for the Firefox web browser, a separate program, or both. It allows researchers to save references from library catalogs, research databases and other websites with a single click. It runs constantly as a plugin in the web browser, which has perhaps become our most essential research tool, so it is always available. It collects saved citations into a personal "library," making them easy to organize and search for later use. A few clicks can turn references in the Zotero library into a bibliography in well over a thousand bibliographic styles. It automatically backs up citations and files to the cloud, making the library accessible from any computer but fully functional offline too.

The 20th-century tool for writers was the typewriter; its 21st-century counterpart is the word processor. In the same way, if a 20th-century tool for researchers was the index card scribbled with citation notes, its 21st-century equivalent is Zotero. It is a personal digital library for the modern researcher: searchable, idiosyncratic to individual needs, shareable, available online and offline. Zotero is free, easy to learn for researchers of all experience levels, powerful, flexible, and quickly becomes an essential part of the researcher's workflow.

There are many programs, called reference management software or reference/citation/bibliography managers, which perform similar functions for the researcher: saving citations, making bibliographies, storing and organizing digital documents. (I'll usually use the generic term "reference manager" when I'm speaking of these tools. In my mind this term includes not only the sense of "reference" as in a works cited list or bibliography, but also as in building and accessing a personal reference collection.) Commercial software in this genre includes EndNote, RefWorks and Procite. They range in function from simplistic to highly technical, in accessibility from effortless to baffling, and in cost from free to hundreds of dollars, or thousands for campus site licenses. I'll attempt to illustrate below what places Zotero among the best of the lot and where it falls on the scales I just laid out. (Short answers: powerful, easy, free.)

Every researcher and every student should use a reference manager program of some kind. Every librarian and every teacher should at least be familiar with reference managers, if not for their own research then so they can understand the tools available to their students and users. Zotero and software like it is no less a research tool than library catalogs, article databases and digital repositories are, and we owe it to our students to show them the best tools for the job.

A Very Brief History: Who Makes Zotero and Why

Zotero is made by researchers for researchers. George Mason University's Center for History and New Media (chnm.gmu.edu) in Fairfax, VA created and develops Zotero. CHNM creates and uses technology tools for education and scholarship in history and the humanities. Zotero is just one of their many projects.

CHNM's team became frustrated with the limitations of commercial reference managers, finding them difficult to use with many catalogs and databases. At the same time, they recognized the opportunity that the open-source web browser Firefox provided. Firefox is designed to allow programs called "add-ons" to augment the way it works, adding new features not intended by the Firefox developers. Add-ons can allow the browser to do seemingly almost anything: save screenshots, control media players, stifle annoying advertisements, or in Zotero's case store bibliographic references. Firefox was the first platform for which Zotero was developed; support for other browsers was first added in early 2011.

They had also noticed a trend in several academic libraries to offer a feature called something like "My Backpack," providing students with online storage space to create personal collections of useful resources. The CHNM team combined these ideas to create a tool that would: run in the browser, which researchers used constantly; work well with a diverse range of databases, catalogs and repositories; and provide a unified "backpack"-style space for users to save their references.

Zotero has received grant support from the Andrew Mellon Foundation, the Alfred P. Sloan Foundation, and the Institute of Museum and Library Services. It has won awards from *PC Magazine*, Northwestern University's CiteFest competition, and the American Political Science Association.

Open-source Software

Zotero is open-source software. This means that the source code—the structure of the Zotero software itself—is available for anyone to download, look at and redistribute freely. Anyone with the requisite knowledge can examine the internal workings of an open-source program, learn how it is made and potentially contribute changes to future versions. Many widely used programs are created under the open-source model: the Firefox web browser, the Linux operating system, the Apache web server (the most widely used web server on the internet), and the OpenOffice application suite, just to name a few examples.

Software made and distributed in this way is also called "free software." This label is slightly ambiguous because of the meanings of the word "free" in English. It can mean "without cost" (*gratis*) or "free to copy and re-use" (*libre*). Some advocates have adopted the acronym FLOSS, "free/libre/open source software" to clarify the meaning. Zotero is FLOSS: "free" in both senses of the word.

Why does all this matter to you as a researcher, teacher or librarian? Several reasons. The first one is obvious: it's free as in *gratis*, no cost, they're giving it away. In the free software community this sense of "free" is called "free as in beer": if a friend gives you a beer just because they're your friend, it costs you nothing. An individual copy of some commercial reference manager software can cost hundreds of dollars. An annual site license for a university can cost many thousands. The benefits of this are obvious! Anything that lessens the strain on students' wallets and library and campus IT budgets is a win.

Zotero is also "free as in speech" (*libre*), free to copy and share without restriction. This has some real practical benefits for both users and support staff. I have worked for two different university libraries, both of which have provided support for a commercial reference manager as well as Zotero. Both universities have a site license for the commercial product, meaning that students and faculty can download it without cost. In order to do so, they have to find the software download page, log in with an ID and password to validate their identity as current students or employees, download and install the software. At my current library, the program in question requires an unintuitive additional step to the installation procedure in order to install it successfully. If this procedure isn't followed correctly, users end up with a non-licensed thirty-day trial version of the software instead. It might be our number one support question, despite the instructions and tutorial video we've posted on our website.

In contrast, we can put a one-click installation link for Zotero anywhere. Because it's free/*libre*, we have no problems with passwords or logins or accidental trial versions. This also means that unlike commercial software, our Zotero-using researchers can take their reference manager with them freely and legally if they graduate or change universities. I would argue that providing free/*libre* tools (and secondarily, teaching our users about them) is very much in line with the mission of libraries and educational institutions.

By their nature, open-source projects have resilience because they are not dependent on a single entity (company, person, university) to survive. CHNM is made up of academic researchers and their main goal is to create a good tool for researchers; Zotero's survival is not contingent on making a profit. They have stable long-term grant funding for Zotero, and we can look forward to many years of development and improvement, but if for some reason George Mason University chose to drop the Zotero project another institution could take up the existing source code and continue to develop it.

The CHNM developers that created Zotero did so with a commitment to open standards. It is designed not only to work with as many online catalogs and databases as possible, but also to import and export to and from as many other different programs as possible. Commercial software often intentionally locks the user into using data in its own proprietary format so that she (or her university) will continue buying future versions of the program to ensure that she can continue to access her files. Zotero makes it easy to share citation files with other software because it can read and write many standard formats used by other programs. If a better reference manager comes along tomorrow (unlikely as that seems) you can reasonably expect to be able to click "export" in Zotero, save your entire library and move it into your new program without a hitch.

This open design also makes Zotero itself extensible. In the same way that Firefox can be enhanced with add-ons like Zotero, Zotero in turn has add-ons that add new features. Because Zotero is open source, programmers can examine its inner workings and find ways to create new uses for it.

Opening the source code of a piece of software also allows an effective strategy for identifying and fixing bugs. Because the code is available to anyone who cares to examine it instead of only a small closed group of developers, the probability of someone being able to spot and repair problems increases dramatically. Open-source advocate Eric S. Raymond calls this principle "Linus's Law" after Linux creator Linus Torvalds: "Given enough eyeballs, all bugs are shallow." As Raymond puts it, "bugs ... turn shallow pretty quickly when exposed to a thousand eager co-developers pounding on every single new release."[1]

Because Firefox checks automatically for updates to all of its add-ons, including Zotero, CHNM can easily push out new versions that correct bugs and add new features, and they do so regularly. The user need only accept the new version when a notification window appears; she need not watch the Zotero website for announcements.

A Word About Firefox

Zotero was first developed for Firefox because it too is open source software. Mozilla, the developers of Firefox, created it with the intention of allowing other programmers to add improvements and features that they didn't anticipate. As I mentioned above, Firefox allows its users to install "add-ons" or "plugins" made by third parties. These add-ons can add remarkable new features to the browser, but this is made possible by the fact that the creators of add-ons have access to Firefox's source code to see how it works. For the first few years of Zotero's existence, it worked only with Firefox, and the Firefox version remains the most mature and stable one for the time being.

For many researchers this isn't a big problem. About a quarter of web users are using Firefox already. I think there may be some overlap between Firefox users and researchers who are more comfortable using technology tools in their work (though that's purely anecdotal and unscientific). This isn't an open-source elitist point of view, and I'm not suggesting that Firefox users are smarter. It's probably just a question of inertia: a new Mac comes with Safari pre-installed and a new Windows computer comes with Internet Explorer (IE). It takes a conscious decision to download and install Firefox or Chrome, and many web users simply don't have a strong enough preference to bother, or the ways in which they use the web aren't significantly affected by choosing one browser over another. Users who choose to take advantage of their browser's more advanced features may come to appreciate the add-on functions of a more extensible browser like Firefox or Chrome.

If you are a librarian who intends to offer Zotero on your student or public computers, you should consider using Firefox, at least for now. Hopefully that won't mean a battle with your administration or IT department—that would probably be an unusual case at this stage in the browser wars. Every campus computer lab and student library computer of my recent experience has already had Firefox installed alongside IE or Safari. Most campus IT professionals and systems librarians recognize the value of having a choice of browsers, the advantages of open source, and the demand for Firefox as a common option. For a few bits of practical advice on implementing Zotero on public workstations, see chapter 7.

Why Use Zotero?

In a way, this is two questions—"Why use a reference manager at all?" and "Why use Zotero in particular?"

The most fundamental reason to use a reference manager is simply that it saves huge amounts of time and effort. Any researcher, whether a student, librarian or professor, always has time constraints. The current research project is never the only plate spinning at any given moment. There are other classes to attend or teach, other papers due, other tasks to complete before the end of the semester. Investing a little time into learning to use a reference manager and incorporating it in to the research process pays off manifold by giving the scholar a complete system for gathering sources, organizing and citing them. Most people can pick up the basics of Zotero in just a few minutes.

I once had a professor specifically ask me not to teach Zotero to her class during a library session because she thought it made the bibliography "too easy." She never used the word "cheat," but she gave me the clear impression that she felt it was something of a lazy shortcut. Of course I acceded to her request—it was her class and I was a guest speaker—but obviously I disagree.

The Association for College and Research Libraries' Information Literacy Competency Standard for Higher Education number 2, performance indicator 5 states that "The information literate student extracts, records, and manages the information and its sources." This indicator's given outcomes include:

a. Selects among various technologies the most appropriate one for the task of extracting the needed information…
b. Creates a system for organizing the information
c. Differentiates between the types of sources cited and understands the elements and correct syntax of a citation for a wide range of resources
d. Records all pertinent citation information for future reference
e. Uses various technologies to manage the information selected and organized[2]

This list of outcomes describes the function of a reference manager nearly perfectly.

A reference manager frees up researchers from much of the mindless clerical process of formatting citations, *so that they can focus on the research itself.* Discovering sources is an important aspect of research. Assessing sources, organizing them, evaluating them and presenting them in an established format are all important aspects of research.

Understanding *why* citations are necessary to the research process is a vital part of learning to be a scholar.

The mechanical exercises of typing out the bibliography, pressing the italics button in the right place and dragging the hanging indent just far enough are not vital scholarly activities. Reference managers can help students learn proper citation practice by providing an efficient way to collect and produce accurate citations, and in fact may encourage them to include more and better citations in their work. In order to use such a tool properly, students still have to learn the function of a bibliography in scholarly writing.

The tools we use in research and writing change with time, and at this point in history many of us have seen this change happening around us during our lifetimes. When I started my undergraduate degree, my university's library still had a card catalog alongside the (green monochrome) online catalog terminals. Readers slightly older than me probably wrote college papers using typewriters rather than word processors, and used print journal indexes rather than article databases.

The writing and searching tools that we all use now are faster, more efficient, and make more resources available to us. They do change the way we work and make research easier. Using them doesn't make us lazy researchers, any more than using a word processor makes me a lazy writer because I don't have to spend time using correction fluid to erase my (frequent) mistakes. We've abandoned old-fashioned tools in the same way that many researchers have abandoned index card notes in favor of a reference manager like Zotero.[3]

Doesn't it keep students from learning how to write bibliographies, if they have a program to "do it for them"? No. This is like asking whether spell-check and grammar-check software relieve the burden of learning to write well, because the software does it. (Students spell-check they're papers, butt your still likely too see them make allot of mistakes.) They will still have to use a style manual in some form, because reference managers don't do the whole job. Even using Zotero, I have to proofread for, and correct, mistakes in capitalization, punctuation and the like before I publish a bibliography, and I always warn students to do the same.

That's the argument for using a reference manager program—any reference manager. Why use Zotero specifically?

Zotero is easy to use. A first-year student can learn the basics of Zotero in ten minutes. It has many advanced features that more sophisticated researchers can appreciate, but the basic "save and cite" function is extraordinarily simple. CHNM often uses the phrase "iTunes-like" to describe the Zotero interface, and it is: clean, logical and familiar to most students. The process of saving citations to the Zotero library is effortless—one click—and consistent across databases and catalogs, unlike some other reference managers that require learning different procedures for each database.

Zotero is free in all the senses discussed earlier. I've already made a case for all the ways in which free software benefits researchers.

Zotero works on many platforms. It works with Firefox and other web browsers. It works with any of the three major operating systems. Its word processor plugin works with Microsoft Word, OpenOffice and NeoOffice. The Firefox version works on every computer and installs with only a couple of clicks. This simplifies the setup process for even very inexperienced computer users. Future versions will work with mobile devices and even via the web without installing any software.

Zotero integrates into the researcher's browser, which is almost always part of the research and writing process. The Firefox version even operates without the need to open a separate application to save and manage citations, annotations, notes and attachments. It's a natural place to include a reference manager, integrating it smoothly into the research process.

Zotero synchronizes the user's library with the Zotero servers. This provides an automatic backup of the researcher's crucial library files. It also takes advantage of the cloud storage provided by CHNM to access the same library on multiple computers and across multiple operating systems. I access my Zotero library, including PDF attachments and notes, on my Windows PC in my office and my Ubuntu Linux netbook at home, without having to copy it manually and keep track of which version is the current one. I can also refer to my library on the web, even on a computer without Zotero installed or on a device like a mobile phone or iPad.

Zotero allows sharing of libraries among classmates, co-authors or other collaborators. Shared libraries can be public or private, and created as open groups which anyone can join or carefully curated by select editors.

Zotero can archive any web page. A single-click function not only saves citation data about a page for the researcher's bibliography, but a copy of the page itself called a "snapshot." Snapshots preserve the full text, graphics, and layout of a page, making it available even if the site goes down, the page is altered or deleted, or the user has no internet connection.

Zotero provides a way to publish bibliographies on the web in a variety of ways, from a simple copy and paste mechanism to plugins for content management systems. The bibliographies that Zotero creates also contain data that Zotero can read, allowing other researchers to capture the same citations to their own libraries.

Zotero encourages others to create new tools. Other institutions have built on CHNM's work to develop plugins that add new features to Zotero. (For a current list, see zotero.org/support/plugins.)

Zotero has an active support community of librarians, faculty, tech evangelists, and programmers. Its official forums (forums.zotero.org) include discussions of features, bugs, uses, bibliographic styles, and more. The Zotero evangelists' listserv (groups.google.com/group/zotero-evangelists) is for librarians and educators who teach or promote Zotero at their institutions.

"Hybrid" Software

In the last few years, cloud computing applications—programs that run entirely on a web server, as opposed to being installed on one's own computer—have become so common as to be unremarkable. It's hard to remember what we did before Gmail and Google Calendar.

Since Zotero works inside the browser window and uses online file storage, many people assume that it too is a cloud application. In fact, it's something of a hybrid. Though tied closely to the web browser, the Zotero software itself (whether the Firefox add-on or the standalone client version) is actually a desktop application, downloaded and installed on the user's computer like any other program. References and attachments are saved on the hard drive. It is easily possible to use Zotero entirely as a local application without taking advantage of any of its online features.

On the other hand, some of the most useful aspects of Zotero involve its cloud integration. The personal Zotero library is created on the hard drive, but setting up automatic cloud-based backup is easy and once set up, automatic. This online synchronization feature also allows easy sharing of references, either privately to the user's other computers or to collaborators anywhere in the world. New and upcoming "Zotero Everywhere" features will allow researchers to use Zotero entirely as a cloud-based application, saving, editing and publishing references via the web without installing a single piece of software.

These hybrid characteristics allow Zotero to take advantages of the best elements of both kinds of software: the reliable availability and fine-tuned customization of desktop applications, and the automatic archiving and easy sharing features of cloud applications.

A Personal Library

Central to the way Zotero and other reference managers work is the idea of the library. In this context we're not talking about library in the sense of a building on campus with bookshelves, but a personal library, a collection of information created by the individual Zotero user for her own research needs.

Thanks to media manager programs like iTunes, most students can grasp this concept quickly when learning Zotero: Your library is comprised of all of the items (music in one case, or citations, notes, and attachments in the other) that you've saved in one place so that you can search it, share it, add to it, annotate it, cite it or otherwise easily use it as you need to. This has many advantages for the researcher, some obvious and some less so.[4]

The personal library is, well, personal. It represents an individually curated collection of sources, not a massive sea of data that includes irrelevancies. This is less pertinent to the undergraduate who needs three sources for an essay in a required first-year composition class, but highly useful for more advanced researchers. Once students reach a level at which they discover their own research interests, whether as undergrad majors or graduate students, they will find themselves revisiting topics in their research and re-using sources as they build on previous projects.

Building a personal library also teaches student researchers about how information is organized in library catalogs and databases. It's one thing for a librarian to teach a student to search a database, but another for the student to create a database of his own as a practical exercise in organizing information for his own needs.

Searching the personal library is fast and easy. Anything saved to a Zotero library is searchable, including the full text of PDF articles and archived web pages. The researcher need not remember the name of the author of "that one really great article" from last year's paper, as long as she can recall a word or two from the title, abstract or subject. Unlike in a commercial research database, the Zotero user can also add notes, tags and other searchable information to any item in the library to make retrieval easier.

In fact the whole library can be organized idiosyncratically, to fit the way you as a researcher prefer to work. Zotero's tags and collections are flexible enough to provide virtual "bookshelves" to group items together, and saved searches can provide self-updating groups of references.

Zotero can create a private archive, not only of bibliographic citations but of any digital objects. Snapshots preserve copies of any web page for offline access or annotation. PDFs, images, text documents, audio files, slide shows, or anything else on your hard drive can be archived and tagged with the information needed for citation and searching.

Beginning undergrads must take classes in varied disciplines, requiring them to produce citations in many different styles over their early academic career: MLA for an English class, Chicago for history, maybe APA for psychology. Saving references to a personal library stores the information in a style-agnostic format, rendering it easy to output in whatever way the professor requires. This makes their references "portable" across classes and more useful to them than simply keeping copies of past papers.

Because the personal library is digital, it can live on the web just as happily as on a hard drive. This means that it is shareable and collaborative in new and exciting ways. Any Zotero library can be made available to other researchers either publicly or privately. Public applications could include publishing bibliographies as a resource for the good of the research community, or to invite commentary on work in progress. Private sharing allows collaborators or classmates to share work across distance in a secure online space.

Scenarios and Personas

In sidebars throughout the book, I'll present scenarios, examples and use cases of how real users might apply the features I'm explaining. To make them a little more concrete, I've chosen to create a few personas, fictional researchers that represent the kinds of Zotero users I teach and help (and learn from) on a regular basis.

Ian: Undergraduate student. Ian is a sophomore majoring in Journalism and going to school full-time. He is taking three courses this semester, one in his major and two others to satisfy the university's general education requirements for a bachelor's degree. Ian's classes this year are proving a little tougher as the research assignments have ramped up a bit from last semester. He's got a lot of conflicting demands on his time and appreciates any tools that will help him get his work done faster. He uses library computers when he can find one available, and his own laptop in his dorm or elsewhere.

Anita: Graduate student. Anita is working on her master's degree in Communication and works for Kate as a research assistant. She is in the midst of writing her thesis and is taking two classes. She's enthusiastic about experimenting with technology and wants to encourage Kate to try some new tools. She is never without her netbook.

Kate: Faculty member. Kate is an associate professor in the Communication department. This semester she is teaching one graduate class and one for undergraduates. She is finishing a journal article and is doing research for a book proposal on the same subject. She doesn't have a lot of time to learn new tools but she's willing to try if it will make her life easier. She does a lot of her research from home where she's less likely to be disturbed but uses her office computer as well.

Nathan: Librarian. Nathan is the subject librarian for the Communication department and the main Zotero instructor and support person on campus. In addition to supporting others' research, he also does his own research and writing. He has an office in the library, but also holds office hours in the Communication department across campus, and often writes on his own laptop at home.[5]

These users and others like them will find Zotero useful as they do research for any number of projects. Over the following chapters we will examine how Zotero can be applied to academic and personal research tasks. (In chapter 6 in particular I am also fortunate to have a number of real-world projects and assignments from Zotero instructors to use as examples.)

Research Uses

Zotero is created primarily as a research tool, and there are several contexts in which it's useful for researchers, such as:

Research papers: The most obvious and clear-cut example for using Zotero is saving sources and creating bibliographies for student research papers. An undergraduate student can learn the basics of how to save citations and turn them into a bibliography in just a few minutes.

Articles and books: Zotero's citation features allow authors to create footnotes or in-text citations and bibliographies automatically. For articles that may need to be reformatted in a style dictated by a journal's editorial guidelines this is a great time saver. Zotero's collections feature allows for easy organizing of citations by chapter for longer works.

Keeping a library of research interests: Once students or more advanced researchers begin discovering and working within a particular research interest, the personal library provides an easy way to track sources for current and future projects and save them for later reference.

Tracking publications: Faculty can keep their own CV up to date by simply saving citations to their own work in their library. Librarians who work with a population of researchers can track their constituents' publications for exhibits or other uses the same way.

Sharing references: Group libraries provide a way to share sources with classmates, students or collaborators. Any Zotero collection can be published to the web, along with the data for other Zotero users to save citations to their own libraries. Professors and research assistants can share libraries with one another.

Tagging images: Zotero provides a mechanism for researchers to add metadata to images: artists, dates, notes and other information that cannot be included in an image file.

Organizing audio: The same goes for audio objects such as recordings of interviews. Saving mp3 files to a Zotero library and attaching them to citation data and even transcripts renders audio recordings easily searchable.

Creative Uses

Zotero's usefulness is not limited to academic research and writing. There are many creative uses for anyone who needs to organize information objects of all kinds. Just to give a few examples:

Collecting book lists (or video lists, or audio, or articles...): One of my Zotero collections is called "Pleasure reading" and is simply a list of novels I want to get around to reading; it consists mostly of citations I saved from Amazon.com. I have another collection called "Look for this," for sources I don't necessarily plan to use in research, but that I want to remember to track down soon.

Bookmarking, personal or shared: There are many social bookmarking applications on the web, but Zotero group libraries allow control over who has read and write access to which sets of bookmarks, and of course Zotero allows file attachments and web snapshots as well.

Citing images: For anyone who uses Creative Commons images in presentations, Zotero allows one-click saving of the citation information and can easily generate a credits list to go in a final slide.[6]

Archiving web pages: Zotero's snapshots feature allows easy backups of any web page for offline viewing or archiving. This can be used for research, or to create a searchable database of any collection of pages—favorite recipes, for example.

Zotero Changes Fast

One of the great things about Zotero is the steady pace at which its developers add new features and release new versions. As I said in the introduction, I expect the material in this book to remain useful for quite some time, but I also expect that there will be additions and improvements by the time you read this that I haven't covered. I still discover new tricks after several years of using and teaching Zotero.

As I was a couple of months into writing this book, the Center for History and New Media announced their new "Zotero Everywhere" features, providing integration into more browsers, enhanced web-based features, and the new Zotero Commons repository. I was both delighted, as an enthusiastic user, and horrified, as an author, since I was now required to radically re-plan and rewrite entire sections of the book and write sections on coming new features as they appeared.

When I started writing this book I thought I knew how to use Zotero—and I did, to a pretty fair degree—but in the course of researching, experimenting with features I'd never used, and talking to other Zotero users I developed a new appreciation for the sophistication and elegance of this software. It's truly a researcher's power tool.

Notes

1. Raymond, "Cathedral and the Bazaar."
2. Association of College and Research Libraries, "Information Literacy Competency Standards for Higher Education."
3. One librarian found that using reference managers encouraged students to use library search tools because the citations were more complete than those saved from Google Scholar: Williams, "When an imploring librarian is not enough."
4. For a useful discussion of the advantages of the personal library, see Hull, Pettifer, and Kell, "Defrosting the Digital Library."
5. It is possible that Nathan's situation contains a few elements from the author's own professional life.
6. Greenhill, "Zotero and saving Flickr images. Wowza!".

Further Reading

Association of College and Research Libraries. "Information Literacy Competency Standards for Higher Education." ACRL, 2000. http://www.ala.org/ala/mgrps/divs/acrl/standards/informationliteracycompetency.cfm.

Center for History and New Media. "Ten Reasons Your Institution Should Adopt Zotero", n.d. http://www.zotero.org/static/download/adopt_zotero.pdf.

Educause. "7 Things You Should Know About Zotero." *Educause*, 2008. http://www.educause.edu/ELI/7ThingsYouShouldKnowAboutZoter/163217.

Greenhill, Kathryn. "Zotero and saving Flickr images. Wowza!" *Librarians Matter*, September 15, 2009. http://librariansmatter.com/blog/2009/09/15/zotero-and-saving-flickr-images-wowza.

Hull, Duncan, Steve R. Pettifer, and Douglas B. Kell. "Defrosting the digital library: Bibliographic tools for the next generation web." *PLoS Computational Biology* 4, no. 10 (October 31, 2008): e1000204.

Morrison, James L., and Trevor Owens. "Next-Generation Bibliographic Manager: An Interview with Trevor Owens." *Innovate: Journal of Online Education* 4, no. 2 (January 1, 2008). http://www.innovateonline.info/index.php?view=article&id=540.

Muldrow, Jason, and Stephen Yoder. "Out of Cite! How Reference Managers Are Taking Research to the Next Level." *PS: Political Science and Politics* 42, no. 1 (January 1, 2009): 167–172.

Puckett, Jason. "Superpower your browser with LibX and Zotero." *College & Research Libraries News* 71, no. 2 (February 2010): 70–97.

Raymond, Eric S. "The Cathedral and the Bazaar: Release Early, Release Often." *The Cathedral and the Bazaar*, 1998. http://www.free-soft.org/literature/papers/esr/cathedral-bazaar/cathedral-bazaar-4.html.

Rosenzweig, Roy. "Historical Note-Taking in the Digital Age | Roy Rosenzweig | August 2007 | OAH Newsletter." *OAH newsletter* 35 (August 2007). http://www.oah.org/pubs/nl/2007aug/rosenzweig.html.

Williams, Mita. "When an imploring librarian is not enough." *New Jack Librarian*, October 6, 2010. http://librarian.newjackalmanac.ca/2010/10/when-imploring-librarian-is-not-enough.html.

CHAPTER 2 Setting Up

So far I've discussed why using Zotero is a good thing and some of the ways in which it's particularly useful. Let's start finding out what using Zotero is actually like. Installing Zotero is very easy and only takes a few clicks.

There are two versions of Zotero , depending on what web browser you use. The original version works only with the Firefox browser; when the distinction matters, I'll refer to it as "Zotero for Firefox." It runs inside the Firefox application and doesn't require running a separate program to work. The newest version, Standalone Zotero, works with other browsers like Chrome and Safari. It's a separate application that runs in its own window.

Once you've installed Zotero, it scans web pages looking for available citations. When it detects that you're on a page that includes a citation of some kind (like a library catalog record, for example), a button appears allowing you to easily save the information to your Zotero library.

Later, as you're writing, you can easily turn those saved citations into a bibliography formatted in whatever bibliographic style you need. There are at least two methods for doing this. Option one is an easy copy and paste system that works with any word processor or text editor, including Google Docs or any web editor. The second method involves installing a toolbar to Word or OpenOffice that allows you to pick citations directly out of your library, and not only creates the bibliography but also the in-text citations or footnotes. (See chapter 4.)

Integrating Zotero into Your Research Process

Before you set up Zotero, consider how using Zotero might affect the way you do research and write. It saves a great deal of time and effort, but it will change the way you work in some ways.

Install Zotero on your research computer(s) before you begin your project. Students often wait until nearly the end of the semester, when they're writing the final bibliography, to begin using a reference manager. Zotero is designed to be involved in the entire research process start to finish. It's nearly effortless to save citations while the initial searches are taking place, but more trouble to install Zotero after writing the paper, go back and re-search the sources and then create the bibliography.

Creating a collection for each project is an easy way to organize sources so they don't get lost in a large Zotero library. Select the collection in your library when you sit down to do research so that all saved references go there automatically. Using tags and saved searches can help keep track of which sources you have obtained and read.[1]

Zotero is not just a save-and-cite application: it's a repository for all your research materials. As you do your research, add notes, PDFs, snapshots, images and tags to your library. Everything you add becomes part of your personal information repository, searchable and organized the way you want it.

Finally, as you write use Zotero to insert citations into your document. It creates the in-text citations or footnotes and builds the bibliography simultaneously. If you notice errors in your citations, correct them in the library (not in your document) so that they will be correct if you cite them in other work. Keep your collection after the project is done so that you can locate your sources for later reference or future projects.

Zotero for Firefox or Standalone Zotero?

Zotero was initially developed for Firefox only, since Firefox was designed for third parties to create new plugins for it that add new features. Early in 2011, CHNM released "Standalone Zotero," a new version that runs as a separate program rather than as a Firefox add-on.[2] What are the differences between the two versions?

- Zotero for Firefox has a single version that runs on any operating system. Standalone Zotero has separate versions for each operating system (Windows, MacOS and Linux).
- Zotero for Firefox requires installing the word processor toolbar as a separate add-on. Standalone Zotero includes word processor toolbars bundled with the software.

- Zotero for Firefox obviously only works with Firefox. Standalone Zotero also works with the Safari and Chrome browsers (in 2011 support for Internet Explorer is planned but not yet available).
- Standalone Zotero requires you to install a "connector" before it can detect and save citations in Chrome and Safari. The connector is a small browser add-on that allows Chrome or Safari to communicate with Zotero. Zotero for Firefox automatically detects citations without any need for a connector.

The two programs can share the same library between them, so it's possible to install and use both. Only one version (Firefox or Standalone) should be running at a time, however, and changes you make in one version won't appear in the other until you close it and restart.

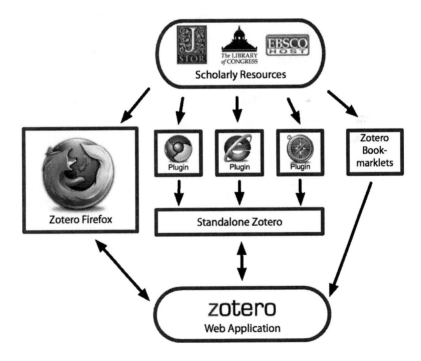

Figure 2.1. Zotero for Firefox and Standalone Zotero, and soon other tools like bookmarklets, provide access to the same personal library. (Image courtesy Center for History and New Media)

In most cases the two versions work more or less identically—the controls, buttons and menus are the same, for example. I typically use Zotero for Firefox in examples unless otherwise noted.

Obviously, you'll need to start by installing Zotero. Let's do it. Install either Zotero for Firefox, or Standalone Zotero, or both, depending on your needs.

Quick Reference: Installing Zotero for Firefox
1. Open zotero.org in Firefox.
2. Click Download on the site, then Allow on the security bar.
3. Click Install Now.
4. (Recommended but optional) Open the Word Processor Plugins page. Choose the appropriate plugin and install as above.
5. Close your word processor if open, and restart Firefox

Installing Zotero for Firefox

Step 1. Open Firefox and go to Zotero.org. Remember that this version of Zotero only works with Firefox. In almost every Zotero class I teach, someone attempts to install it using Internet Explorer no matter how many times I repeat the instructions to open Firefox. If you're teaching a Zotero workshop, plan to walk around for some hands-on assistance during the installation steps.

Step 2. Click the large red "Download" button at the top right. At the top of the page, Firefox will open a notification that says "Firefox prevented this site (www.zotero.org) from asking you to install software on your computer." Don't worry! This is a standard warning that you'll see any time you install a Firefox add-on. It's just alerting you to the fact that you've just clicked a link that will install a browser extension. Click the Allow button to continue. In older Firefox versions (pre-4.0) this alert message is sometimes easy to overlook because it's not in an eye-popping color. If you're teaching, don't be surprised if some students don't notice it.

Step 3. A new window called "Software Installation" appears. **Click the Install Now button** to install Zotero. This button counts down for five seconds from "Install (5)" before it allows you to click it, to encourage users to read the window before agreeing to install software.

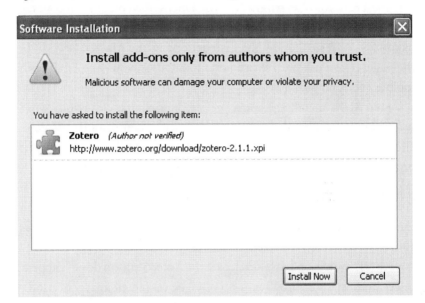

Figure 2.2. Installing Zotero for Firefox

The Software Installation window will close, and the Add-ons window will open and display a progress download is finished, a "Restart Firefox" button appears at the top right of the Add-ons window. Don't click it yet, though; we can save a step by installing both Zotero components at the same time.

Step 4. Go back to Zotero.org. Below the Download button you'll see a link that says "**Download word processor plugins.**" Click this link to go to the "word processor plugin installation" page (zotero. org/support/word_processor_plugin_installation). This page includes the various toolbars that allow you to insert Zotero citations and bibliographies into your documents, which we'll look at more closely in chapter 4.

Zotero for Firefox only has one version that works with all operating systems, but there are separate versions of the word processor plugin depending on which program you use: there is a version for Word for Windows, one for Word for Mac OS, and so on. Scroll down until you see the name of your word processor (Word or OpenOffice). Each has its own link labeled, for example, "**Install the Word for Windows Plugin**" (or "the Word for Mac plugin" or "the OpenOffice plugin," of course). Mac users should install an additional plugin called PythonExt linked from this page; just follow the instructions in the Mac OS section of the page. If you use both Word and OpenOffice, you can install both toolbars with no problems.

Step 5. To install the word processor toolbars, close your word processor and follow the same steps you did when installing Zotero: click the appropriate Install link, click Allow, Install, and wait for the progress bar. This time, **click the Restart Firefox button**. As you'd expect, this will restart Firefox. (Restart your word processor too, if it was open.) When it opens again, you should see the word Zotero in the bottom right corner of the browser window. Your browser now has 100% more Zotero available.

Installation problems—such as if the Zotero button doesn't appear in the bottom of the browser—can often be corrected just by reinstalling Zotero and restarting the browser. If you're installing the Firefox version of Zotero, make sure you're actually in Firefox, or it won't work.[3]

Like all Firefox add-ons, Zotero for Firefox and its toolbars are self-updating. Firefox periodically checks for new versions to all of your installed add-ons, including Zotero, and will prompt you if it detects a new version available. I recommend immediately installing

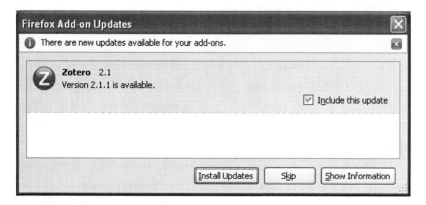

Figure 2.3. Firefox prompts you to update when a new version of the Zotero add-ons are available.

any new Zotero versions since they often include important bug fixes, style revisions or translator updates.

Firefox will also prompt you to install new versions of the word processor toolbars when available. Make sure your word processor is closed before you install the new versions.

Installing Standalone Zotero

Standalone Zotero is the new version of Zotero that runs as a separate application, not as a Firefox plugin (it's a "standalone" application, whereas Zotero for Firefox runs as part of the browser). This allows Zotero to work with other browsers like Chrome and Safari. Installation is a bit different, but once installed the two versions of Zotero work almost identically. The main difference is that Zotero for Firefox runs in a "pane" in the Firefox browser window that can be hidden or displayed as needed, while Standalone Zotero runs in its own application window. Standalone Zotero also requires a small plugin—a "connector"—to allow it to save items from browsers other than Firefox. Zotero for Firefox and Standalone Zotero can be installed on the same computer, and either one can save data to the same library, but only one of the two programs can run at a time.

There are separate versions of Standalone Zotero for each operating system. The appropriate word processor plugins are included with each version, unlike Zotero for Firefox.

Step 1. Go to zotero.org/support/standalone and **download the version of Zotero for your operating system**. (Details of installing the application will depend on your OS; check with your IT help desk if you need advice on how to install software on your system.)

Step 2. Download the connector for your browser from the Zotero Connectors list. Just click the link labeled "Zotero Connector for Chrome" or "Zotero Connector for Safari" and when prompted confirm that you want to proceed with the installation. Like the Firefox version, downloading and installing only takes a few seconds.

Step 3. Run the Standalone Zotero program. The software will ask you whether to import your settings from Zotero for Firefox if you have installed the Firefox version already. In most cases you'll want to answer yes; this allows the two programs to save items to the same library. If you choose "no" or "custom data directory" Standalone Zotero and Zotero for Firefox will each have their own separate library.

If the two programs share a library, only one program can be active at a time. If you attempt to run Standalone Zotero while Firefox with the Zotero extension is running (or vice versa), a warning will appear advising you to close one program before opening the other.

At this point, Zotero for Firefox is the more mature and stable version, and in much wider use. Because of this, most of the examples in this book (and most Zotero documentation on the web) assume that you're using Zotero for Firefox. Fortunately, the two versions behave almost identically: the Standalone Zotero window looks and acts exactly like the Zotero pane in Firefox. All the buttons are the same, and the combination of Standalone plus connector will provide the same functions that the Firefox version does.

The Zotero Pane

Click the Zotero button in the bottom right corner of Firefox to open up your Zotero library pane. (You can use control-alt-Z in Windows or Linux, or command-shift-Z in Mac, as a keyboard shortcut.) The Standalone Zotero window looks exactly like the Firefox Zotero pane: all the buttons and functions are the same. When you open this pane it fills the bottom section of your browser, leaving the top to display your current web page as normal. Drag the top edge up and down to adjust the size of the pane. Press the Toggle Tab Mode button, in the top right corner of the pane between the green circular arrow and the Close button, to fill the entire window and run in a browser tab. Zotero for Firefox continues to run while Firefox is open, whether the pane is visible or not. Open and close the Zotero pane as needed while you work.

The Zotero interface is designed to remind users of iTunes, a program that most people find intuitive and familiar. It's divided into three columns:

In the left column you can see "My Library" near the top next to a small box icon. Clicking this icon will show all the references you've saved. This area will also include collections (subsets of your library like folders or playlists) and group libraries that you share with other

Zotero users. Libraries are indicated by brown box icons, and collections with yellow folder icons (blue for Mac users).

Below this is the tag selector, showing all the "tags" attached to the library or collection you're viewing. At the moment this area is probably empty.

Click "My Library" in the left column. The middle column of the Zotero pane shows a list of all of the items in your library. If you select a collection or a group library (more about these later), Zotero will show all the items contained in whichever collection or library you've selected. An "item" in Zotero is a reference, a note, a snapshot, a web link—any single thing that you have saved in your Zotero library. Usually this means a reference like a book or article citation, but an item can also be a PDF file or any number of other things. Items can be attached to other items: a plus or minus sign (or a triangle icon on some operating systems) appears next to items with attachments. Clicking the plus sign or triangle shows the attachments, and clicking the minus sign (or triangle again) hides them.

If you've just installed Zotero for the first time, the only item in your library is a link to the Zotero "Quick Start" guide, which is a useful page to add to your browser's bookmarks too.

From left to right, the three columns go from libraries and collections, to lists of items, to an individual item. When you click a library or collection in the left column, it displays its contents in the middle; when you click an item in the middle column, it displays details on the right. Click the Quick Start guide (or another item if you have others in your library). In the right column, you'll see the bibliographic information Zotero records about this website. You can edit any field—title, author, date, and so on—just by clicking once on the text in the right column and typing over it.

A row of buttons spans the top of the Zotero pane. We'll examine their functions in some detail through the next few chapters.

The best way to learn Zotero is to dive in and try it. The first thing you'll need to do is learn how to put items into your library by saving some citations. The next chapter will show you how to build your library.

Notes

1. Mullen, "How to Create a Work Flow in Zotero."
2. At the time this book went to press, CHNM had just released the alpha (early test) version of Standalone Zotero. There have likely been improvements and additional features added by the time you read this; check the Zotero website for updates.
3. The first time you reload Firefox after installing Zotero, the "Welcome to Zotero" page opens in the browser. Library IT staff who are creating a disc image for public computers may want to restart Firefox again before making the image, or this page may come up on every imaged computer every time Firefox starts.

Further Reading

Center for History and New Media. "Zotero—Quick Start Guide", 2009. http://www.zotero.org/documentation/quick_start_guide.

Mullen, Lincoln. "How to Create a Work Flow in Zotero." *Backward Glance*, August 28, 2009. http://lincolnmullen.com/2009/08/28/how-to-create-a-work-flow-in-zotero/.

Puckett, Jason. "Zotero [GSU Library guide]", 2011. http://research.library.gsu.edu/zotero.

CHAPTER 3 Creating your Library

To summarize as broadly as possible for a moment, Zotero has two major functions: putting "stuff"—citations, attachments, notes—into your library, and getting "stuff"—bibliographies and reports—out, in the format you need. This chapter covers putting stuff in: saving, entering and organizing your references in your Zotero library.

Saving Citations: The Basics

Zotero allows you to save citations from most library catalogs and article databases, and some other sites, with a single click. Open your library's catalog in Firefox. (I've chosen to use WorldCat, worldcat.org, in my examples here. Non-librarian readers may not be aware of WorldCat; it searches many library catalogs at once and is a very handy research tool.)

Try out a search: author, title, subject—it doesn't matter as long as you get a list of results in your browser. Click on a single item so that you're looking at the catalog record, or descriptive information, for a book.

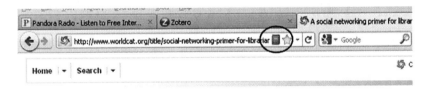

Figure 3.1. The capture icon appears at the right end of the browser's address bar.

Now look at the address bar at the top of your browser. At the rightmost end of the address bar you should see a small blue book icon (figure 3.1). This is a "capture icon," Zotero's indication to you that it has detected a bibliographic citation on this page that it can save to your library. Click the blue book and watch the bottom right corner of the browser window. A small dialog box appears that says "Saving Item…" with the title of the book (figure 3.2).

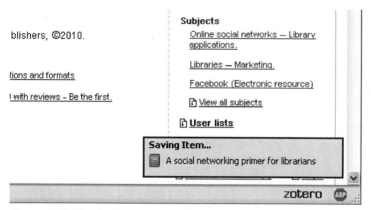

Figure 3.2. The Saving Item notification appears in the bottom right corner of the browser.

Open the Zotero pane to view your library. It now contains the citation you just saved, the name of the catalog from which you saved all this information, and a note that you saved it on today's date (figure 3.3). (You'll download more or less information depending on what library catalog you used, but it should almost always include the essentials you need for a bibliography: author, title, publisher, place and date.) Use the scroll bar on the right side to see the entire citation.

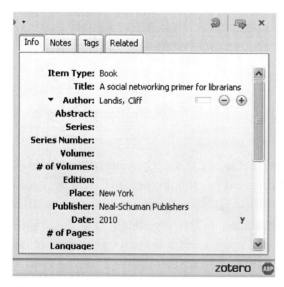

Figure 3.3. The book citation saved in Zotero.

Figure 3.4. When viewing a list of items, the capture icon looks like a folder. Click it to save several citations at once.

If you're on a page containing a *list* of search results instead of a single item, Zotero indicates this fact by changing the capture icon to a folder (figure 3.4). Go back to the search results page (you can probably just press Back on your browser). The blue book button changes to a yellow folder capture icon. Zotero is indicating that there are several citations available to save. You will usually see this icon appear when viewing a list of search results.

Click the folder button. A list of all the references on this page opens, each with a checkbox (figure 3.5). Check off each item you want to save to your library (or use the Select All button) and click OK. The Saving Items dialog will appear in the bottom right again. If you are saving several references this will take a few seconds, so be patient. Each title will appear in the Saving Items popup notification as Zotero saves it to your library.

The reference will be saved to whatever library or collection you currently have selected in your Zotero pane, whether the pane is visible

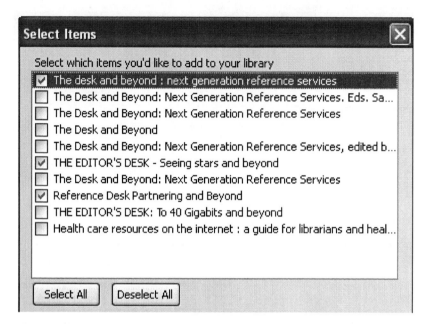

Figure 3.5: Check off each item you want to save from a list of search results.

Off-campus Proxies

A proxy server is a tool that allows off-campus researchers to access restricted library resources like article databases. When you log into JSTOR or EBSCO Academic Search from home via your library's website, you're using the proxy server.

When you use Zotero from off campus, it detects when you log into a database via a proxy server and offers to route you through your library's server automatically in future.

For example, if you go to your library's website to connect to JSTOR, Zotero pops up a window asking whether you want future JSTOR connections to automatically go through your university library. Click "Add proxy" to activate this feature.

This allows you to type jstor.org into your browser to log in and connect to JSTOR next time, instead of having to go to your library's site first.[1]

or not. In other words, open Zotero with control-alt-Z or by clicking the Zotero button in the bottom right of your browser. If you select My Library at left, all new references you save will go into your library but not into a collection. If you select a collection, newly saved references will go into that collection (and into My Library as well, since it includes all items in your collections too). If you select a group library, new saved references will be stored there. Close Zotero and the location for new references won't change until you open Zotero and select a different library or collection.

Those are the basic steps to save citations from almost any catalog or article database. It's incredibly easy: search as usual, and when you need to save citations click the icon in the address bar. If you try the process again in an article database, the only difference you should notice is that Zotero indicates article citations with a white page icon instead of a blue book icon. (If you don't have easy access to an article database, try Google Scholar, scholar.google.com.)

Zotero uses other icons to indicate different types of references: the blue book and white article page that we've already seen, an iPod icon to indicate audio recordings, filmstrip to indicate visual recordings, a "painting" icon for artwork or images, and a blue page for websites, for example. (See figure 3.6 for a partial list.) Zotero uses these same icons in your library list, so you can tell at a glance what type a given reference is.

Figure 3.6. A partial list of capture icons for various reference types. These icons appear both in your browser's address bar and in your Zotero library.

That's almost everything you need to know about how to save citations. I always advise researchers to double-check the information in their saved citations, especially when using a particular catalog or database with Zotero for the first time. Zotero usually does a good job of saving the information correctly, but occasionally I find missing information, or information in the wrong field of the citation, such as a publisher name in the Place field. Also, Zotero saves title capitalization exactly as it appears in the online resource, so if an article's title is capitalized incorrectly in the database it will be saved the same way in your Zotero library. You can correct any problems in your saved references just by clicking on the text that needs to be changed and typing over it. For capitalization problems, right-click the title and choose "lower case" or "Title Case" from the Transform Text menu

Students sometimes have the impression that Zotero saves references in a particular bibliographic style like MLA or Chicago, and ask how to choose the style they need for their papers. The answer is that these references aren't being saved in *any* style. Zotero saves each field, or element of the citation like title or author, to its database and doesn't apply any styles until you create a bibliography. (Chapter 4 describes how to do that.)

How Does it Work?

Without getting too technical, let's pause for a moment to examine what Zotero is doing and how it can tell when you're looking at a citation.

Every time you view a web page in your browser, Zotero scans it. It's looking for what librarians call "metadata"—information about a citation, like title, author, and publisher—in a form that it can recognize. The metadata is encoded into the web page, invisible to the human eye.

If Zotero can recognize the metadata on a page, it notifies you with an icon in the address bar as you've already seen. It shows a single-item capture icon (like the blue book) if it detects a single citation, and the folder button if it detects multiple citations, usually on a page of search results. (There are a few sites for which Zotero can detect a single item citation but not a results list or vice versa.)

Every website provides its metadata in a slightly different format (though that's a bit of an oversimplification: for example, all EBSCO databases use the same format, and many sites use the same standard forms of metadata). Zotero uses pieces of code called site translators to interpret all these different formats and keep track of the correct way to interpret the contents of given sites. There are translators built into Zotero for most library catalogs and research databases. Zotero updates include updates to translators as well, so there is no need to download new translators yourself.

A few notable sites for which Zotero has translators—meaning sites from which you can easily save citations to Zotero—include:

- Amazon.com
- Flickr
- Google Scholar
- Google Books
- The *New York Times*
- Wikipedia
- YouTube
- ...as well as most library catalogs and most article databases.

A longer list is available at zotero.org/translators. This list, maintained by the Zotero developers, is not 100% complete because there are many sites that work with Zotero even though they have no site translator explicitly written for them: If a site uses a standard metadata format (one format used by many sites is called COinS, for example), Zotero can recognize and download citations.

Not all of the sites on this short list, or the much longer one on the Zotero website, are what we might think of as traditional research tools like library catalogs. Zotero can save image citations from Flickr or video citations from YouTube as easily as article citations from Academic Search Complete or PubMed, and it saves book citations from Amazon as well as from the Library of Congress catalog.[2]

It Didn't Work!

There are a couple of cases in which this otherwise effortless process of saving citations might fail.

Astute readers may notice that I have carefully said that Zotero works with *most* catalogs and databases. The fact is that there are a few catalogs and article databases with which it doesn't work, though the Zotero developers and volunteers add new sites all the time.

If the site you're using simply doesn't show a Zotero capture icon when you view a citation or list of search results, there are two options that might still allow you to save the citation.

First, many databases and catalogs have an "export" or "save" feature offering the user the ability to send citations directly to reference manager software. Zotero is rarely explicitly named in the list of compatible programs, but this feature usually works with Zotero anyway. Look for an option labeled something like "Export to EndNote or Reference Manager" or "Export to RIS." RIS (Research Information Systems, the name of the company that developed the format) is a standard format for citation data that most reference managers, including Zotero, can import. Avoid any "Export to RefWorks" choice: this generally won't work.[3]

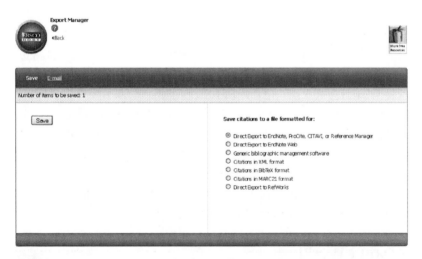

Figure 3.7. Export screen from a database. The export to EndNote or RIS format will usually work, and export to Refworks usually won't.

If the database or site from which you need to save citations lacks either a Zotero capture icon *or* a compatible export feature, the best option may be simply to find the citation in a different database. For example, although Lexis-Nexis is listed on Zotero's compatible translator list, I have never been able to successfully capture or export a Lexis-Nexis citation to Zotero. When I need to save newspaper citations from Lexis-Nexis, I just copy the article title, open a new browser window to ProQuest Newspapers, paste the title into the search box, and capture the citation from ProQuest. (Sorry, legal researchers: at this writing, Westlaw doesn't work either). When using a library catalog that isn't Zotero-friendly, the best option is often to switch over to Worldcat.org or Amazon.com to capture the needed citations.

The second failure case is when Zotero displays a capture icon, but can't actually save the citation. When the user clicks the capture button Zotero shows an error message and suggests consulting the list of known translator problems.

This usually happens when a site that previously worked with Zotero changes its metadata format, temporarily "breaking" the Zotero capture function. Zotero detects the metadata on the page, and "thinks" it knows how to save it, but because the site has changed Zotero cannot actually save the reference. (As I wrote this chapter, EBSCOhost, the company that produces many of the research databases I use most often, changed the format of its data. My attempted citation captures with Zotero either failed or didn't show an icon at all, seemingly switching back and forth on a daily basis. This situation lasted a few weeks.)

The short-term workaround for this problem is to use one of the methods I recommended above: either use the database's native export function instead of the Zotero capture icon, or if possible grab the citation from a different database. The actual solution takes a bit longer: report the problem in the Zotero discussion forum if no one already has, and be patient. The Zotero developers usually catch up with these problems quickly, often within a couple of weeks. The next Zotero update will probably include a new version of the translator to correct the problem.

Saving Citations: Web Pages

All of the above applies to capturing citations from sites like research databases, catalogs, online encyclopedias and booksellers—sites that include that vital metadata for Zotero to scan and capture. Researchers often need to cite sites that Zotero's translators don't automatically detect and pages that don't include citation metadata: what we might call "plain old web pages" (as opposed to a citation page from a catalog or database). Fortunately Zotero is prepared to handle this situation; saving a web page as a reference just takes an extra click and probably a little editing.

First, browse to a web page that you want to save in your library. In my classes for journalism students I often go to CNN.com and choose any story from the front page as an example. Zotero doesn't display a capture icon for any pages on this site, but it's still possible to save the citation.

Open Zotero. Look at the row of buttons above the middle panel and note the button just above the column header "Title" in your library. It's a light blue page icon with a tiny green plus sign: "Create new item from current page."

Click this button to save a new Zotero reference from the page currently displayed. A new item of the type "Web Page" will appear in your library. Zotero can save the URL, the title (from the page's <title> tag, the same text that appears in your browser's title bar), the date of access, and a "snapshot" of the page: a copy of the entire page saved as an attachment. More about that below.

There are a few key pieces of information that Zotero can't save automatically in web page citations. After you've captured the citation, look at the Info tab in the right panel. It lacks an author name, a date of publication, a *website* title (as distinct from the *page's* title), and possibly other information that your bibliography might need.

Fortunately you can add this information yourself by clicking on the missing element and just typing or copying and pasting it in. If you saved a news story as in the example, the site probably gives an author name and publication date which you can paste in. The page's title sometimes needs editing too: CNN stories include an extraneous "—CNN.

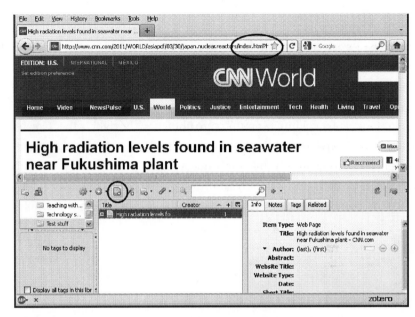

Figure 3.8. Saving a web citation. Notice that there's no Zotero capture icon in the address bar, but you can save the citation using the Create New Item button at the top of the Zotero pane. Add needed information like author and date by typing it into the right column.

com" in the page title that I would delete to make the bibliography a bit neater, and I add "CNN" or "CNN.com" as the website title instead.

(One hidden trick for websites and other online sources: clicking the URL label in the right column—not the actual URL, but the word "URL" itself—will open that site in your browser.)

Add by Identifier: Saving Citations by Number

Some types of references have unique ID numbers that can be used to locate them easily online. Most books have International Standard Book Numbers (ISBN), codes that booksellers use to identify a specific edition of a specific title (you can see one on the barcode on the back of this book if you're reading the physical print edition). Many on-line documents have a Digital Object Identifier (DOI), a number like "doi:10.1000/182" that can be included in citations as a permanent way to locate an object even if its URL changes. Each article in the PubMed database for medical researchers includes a PubMed Identifier (PMID) for similar purposes.

If you have a book with an ISBN or an article with a DOI or PMID, Zotero can automatically capture all its citation information for you. Above the center column of your Zotero library, to the right of the "Create New Item From Current Page" button we used in the previous section, you'll see a small button that looks like a magic wand. Click the wand and type or copy and paste the number. Zotero will search for a few seconds, then your book or article citation should appear in your library.

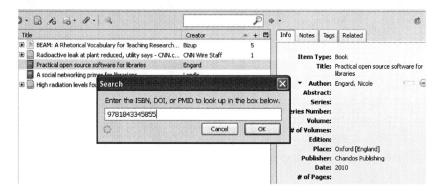

Figure 3.9: Use the magic wand button and enter an ISBN, DOI, or PMID number to automatically download a citation.

To find your item, Zotero searches the appropriate database for the type of number you enter (WorldCat for ISBNs, the DOI resolver CrossRef for DOIs, and PubMed for PMIDs) and downloads the citation just like it would any other reference.

Some DVDs and CDs have ISBNs, and if they're listed in WorldCat this feature will work for them as well. Zotero always saves them as item type Book, so (as always) check your saved citations and make corrections as needed.

Retrieving Citations for PDFs

Zotero can automatically retrieve citation data for *some* PDF documents by searching for them in Google Scholar. This is useful for researchers with large collections of saved articles who are using a reference manager program for the first time.

Drag PDFs into the Zotero pane—open the Zotero window, and drag some PDFs from your desktop into the center column. The files will be copied into the Zotero library, but as standalone items, not citations.

Next, select and right-click the PDFs inside the Zotero library. From the popup menu, choose "Retrieve Metadata for PDF." This (rather unintuitive menu item) will cause Zotero to search Google Scholar for matches. Zotero creates citations for any PDFs it can match, attaching the original file to the new citation.

Creating and Editing Citations

Sometimes it's not practical to search for an item online in order to add it to your library. You may have the book in your hand and not want to bother looking it up in a catalog. You could be citing an item that doesn't appear in any online search tools, like a personal interview, an image or an unpublished manuscript. There are easy options for handling either case.

At the top of the center column of the Zotero pane, above the "Title" label in your library, you'll see a green plus sign button: the New Item button. (Zotero uses the common convention of using a green plus sign on any "create new something" buttons. In this case it's the whole button; in other cases it appears in the bottom right corner of buttons.) Click this button to create a new empty reference in your library. A menu appears with the most common reference types listed first: Book, Book Section, Document (a generic "catch-all" reference type) and a few different kinds of articles. A "more" choice appears at the bottom of the list, giving access to most of the other reference types. Choose the item type you need (we'll use Book in this example) and a blank reference of that type will appear in your library. If you need to change an item's type, click it to see a drop-down menu with all possible types and select the one you want.

Your new item's information appears in the right column ready for you to edit. The left side of any citation's information consists of labels (or "fields") like Title, Author, and Publisher; these cannot be changed (except for Author , which can be changed to Editor or a few other choices). The right side, which is blank in your new citation, contains information that can be edited just by clicking next to the label. Click in the blank next to the label Title and type in the title of a book.

Press Tab to move to the next field, the Author's last name. Type the last name here, then tab to the first name and fill that in. You can fill in the entire citation just by tabbing through. Skip anything that doesn't apply: if your book doesn't have a series title or volume number, it's fine to leave those fields blank. When finished entering information, just click outside the text areas or press Enter.

Editing an existing citation works the same way as typing a new one. To edit any citation, whether one Zotero has saved or one you've typed in yourself, click on the text and make your changes. Press Enter or click outside the text again when done. Zotero automatically saves your changes as you edit or create items.

Each item type has some variation in the fields it includes. Change your book to a journal article by clicking the label Book and scrolling down the menu to choose Journal Article. Zotero adds a Publication field, Volume and Issue numbers, and Journal Abbreviation. (You'll also notice the icon change to a white page image in your library list in the center column.)

Look back at the Author label again. This field has a few extra buttons because of the varying types of "authors" you might encounter. The Author label is the only label that can be changed: click the word Author and you'll see other choices like Editor, Translator or Contributor. Change this as needed. (I'll continue to call this field Author for simplicity, but your reference may have an Editor or another label here.)

The Author field includes a last name and first name, but some works may not list an individual's name as author: a report might simply be credited to the U. S. Department of Education or to Georgia State University (this kind of author, an organization or other non-individual entity, is called a corporate author). To the right of the author's first name field you'll see a small white oblong button. Press that to change the two "last" and "first" fields to a single name field or back again. Use the single field for a corporate author name and the last-first fields for individual names.

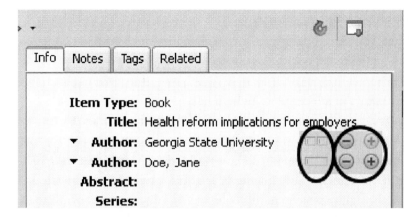

Figure 3.10. Use the small buttons to the right of author names to switch between a corporate author and an individual with first and last names. Use the plus and minus buttons to add or remove additional authors.

To the right of that button are two more: a plus and a minus sign. These buttons allow you to add additional Author fields. This is useful in several cases: many journal articles are written by multiple authors; a book may list authors, an editor, translator and other contributors; and a video recording citation may list a director, producer, screenwriter and actors. As you might have guessed, click the plus button to add as many additional authors as you need and the minus button next to any author to remove it.

One common correction you may need to make in database citations saved by Zotero is capitalization. Most library catalogs provide titles in sentence case: first letter and proper nouns are capitalized but all else is lowercase. Some article databases provide titles in all caps. You'll need to adjust the capitalization appropriately to the citation style you need (Zotero leaves capitalization correction up to you, since it can't tell what words are proper nouns).

Right-click the text of a title in your library to see the Transform Text menu, which can set the title to Title Case (all first letters capitalized, except words like "and" and "the") or to all lowercase. Make any further edits you need by hand.

Organizing your Library

When you view your library or a collection (see below), its contents show in the center column of the Zotero pane. Several labels are visible at the top of this column: Title, Creator, and + (the plus sign indicates the number of attachments an item has).

You can sort your library in order by clicking any of these labels. For example, click Title to sort alphabetically by title or the plus sign to sort by number of attachments. Clicking the label again will reverse the sort.

To change the labels that appear at the top of the center column, click the rightmost icon in this column. This displays a list of all labels to choose from, with the currently displayed labels checked. Choose the labels you wish displayed by clicking them to toggle them on or off. Choose Restore Defaults at the bottom of the list to reset the column labels to Title, Creator and + again.

Collections

Since citations are so easy to save, a Zotero library can quickly get very large. Fortunately, organizing references into lists or "collections" is easy. A collection is simply a list of library items, such as all the references for a particular project or class. You can create as many collections as you need, and an item can be in more than one collection at a time if needed.

To create a collection, click the "New Collection" button at the top left of the Zotero pane. It looks like a yellow folder with a tiny green plus icon. Type a name for the new collection and press Enter or click OK.

Your new (empty) collection will be selected automatically when you create it. Select any collection by clicking it in the left column. When a collection is selected, any new items you create or save will go into the new collection. At any time you can view your entire library, including all items in collections, by clicking My Library again.

You can also add items to a collection by clicking them in the center column and dragging them to the collection in the left column. If you try to drag items into a collection that already includes them, you'll see a "no" circle/slash icon. To see whether an item is already in one or more collections, select it by clicking, and hold down the Control key. The collections that contain that item will highlight in yellow.

Get a list of all items that aren't in *any* collections by right-clicking your library and choosing "Show Unfiled Items" from the menu.

Although collections are represented with a folder icon just like a directory on your hard drive, a collection does not behave exactly like a usual computer folder. A file on your computer can only exist in one folder at a time. A Zotero item can exist in multiple collections simultaneously. A collection is simply a list of items, and items can be on more than one list: for example, I can create a "Georgia history" collection and a "Civil War" collection and include a citation in both collections without making a duplicate of it.

You can create collections within collections by right-clicking any collection and choosing "New subcollection." You can also rename or remove a collection via the right-click menu. Removing a collection does not delete the items it contains from your library, it just removes the list.

I find it useful to make a collection for each topic or project for which I am doing research. I have a "Pleasure reading" collection for novels I want to remember to read someday; I save citations from Worldcat or Amazon as I come across interesting books (which takes up much less space than a stack of books on my nightstand). Since I provide help for Zotero users, I also have a "Test stuff" collection to which I save citations for demonstrations or troubleshooting, so that I can easily find those items to delete when I finish.

Tags

If you have ever shared photos on a site like Flickr or Facebook you're familiar with the concept of "tagging" items: adding keywords—"tags"—to make them searchable. Librarians, of course, have been tagging information sources since long before computers existed, in the form of subject headings, author names and other information added to catalog records to make books and articles easier to find.

Tagging items in a Zotero library serves the same purpose: tags simply add additional information to a library item for easier searching, grouping or organizing. While labels like authors, titles and publisher names are pre-determined, tags are one form of metadata—extra, searchable information attached to the item—that the researcher can customize herself according to her own needs and preferences. Tags will never appear in the bibliography; they exist solely to aid searching the library. Citations are the only type of item that can include tags.

Select any citation in your library and click the Tags tab in the right column. Any existing tags on this item display here. You can add your own tags just by clicking the Add button and typing a word or phrase to describe the item, like "monkeys" to describe a book on monkeys, or "English 101" to tag an item you'll be using in a particular class. Remove a tag by clicking the minus button next to it.

It is helpful to use consistent tags to describe similar items so that you can be sure to catch all similar items with a single search. For example, if I tag some items for my class "English 101" and others "engl101," searching for "english" will miss the latter tag. (Librarians are already familiar with this practice of using a "controlled vocabulary," which simply means using the same set of consistent terms to aid searching.) Zotero assists with this by suggesting existing terms that match what you have already typed as you enter tags. You can choose an existing term by clicking one of the suggestions as they appear.

You may find that some of your citations already have tags: by default, Zotero saves subject headings and keywords from catalog and database records as tags. You can disable this behavior if you prefer by choosing Preferences from the action (gear) menu; on the General tab, uncheck the box for "Automatically tag items with keywords and subject headings."

At the bottom of the left column you'll see a tag browser and search box. The tag browser, the list of tags below your collections, shows the tags for all the citations currently displayed in the center column. If you select My Library, the browser shows all the tags in the library. Selecting a collection displays only the tags in that collection. Click any tag to show only the citations tagged with that term. Select more tags to narrow the match further. (On small screens, the tag browser shows only a small fraction of the entire set of tags. Use the mouse wheel to scroll up and down or drag the top edge of the tag browser up to enlarge it.) Click "Deselect all" to clear your selections and show the entire library/collection again. The search box allows you to search for terms to select in the tag browser.

The most obvious way to apply tags is by subject, creating tags that describe the content of the item: "monkeys," "cystic fibrosis," or "fantasy fiction." Tags can be personalized and idiosyncratic, however, so feel free to apply them as needed. I have already suggested tagging items with the name of a course or project, like "English 101," but tags can also be added (and deleted) to keep track of their status in your workflow: "needed," "ordered," "obtained," or "read." History students might need to tag sources "primary" or "secondary." Sources for a thesis could be tagged "chapter 1" and so on. (Collections can also be used in many of these ways—each researcher can decide what works best for him.)

Related Items

Library items can be linked to each other by marking them as "related." Related items are any items that you choose to indicate as relevant to one another in some way.

To mark items as related, click an item's Related tab (next to the Tags tab) in the right column and click Add. This brings up a window to browse and select another item from the library. Selecting the item marks both items as related to one another, adding a link to each other's Related tab. Clicking an item on the Related tab navigates back and forth between items quickly.

You might want to mark all the items in a series as related, for example. Other uses could include marking author biographies or other secondary sources related to their primary work, marking all items for a particular project as related, or alternate editions of a given work.

Attachments, Notes and Snapshots

So far we've examined all the ways to put citations into your library, but Zotero can store and organize almost any file on your computer, not just bibliographic references.

Think of your Zotero library like a file box. You already know how to put references, like index cards containing your citation information, into the box: save it from a catalog, database, or other website, or type it by hand. These references are one type of item in your library, like digital note cards.

The file box can store other kinds of items as well: any file you have on your hard drive can be stored as an item in your Zotero library. You can also "attach" these items to your references, like stapling a document to a note card. Probably the most common use for this feature is to save an article citation and attach a PDF copy of the article, so that the citation and article are stored together.

Zotero items can include:

- Citations
- Files: often PDFs, but also images, documents, audio files or any other digital file
- Notes: you can type your own notes, and many saved citations include notes containing text that doesn't go into any of the existing Zotero fields
- Web links: this includes the URL and the date you created the link
- Snapshots: copies of a web page that include graphics, your own highlighting and annotations.

Attachments

Any of these items above can either exist independently or be attached to citations. An item that is attached to a citation remains associated with it: if you move or delete a citation with attachments, you also move or delete the attachments. A citation with attachments has a plus sign or arrow next to it in your library list. Click the arrow or plus to show or hide an item's attachments.

Zotero sometimes refers to the attachment as the "child" and the item to which it is attached as the "parent." An item that is not attached to a citation is a "standalone" item.

View any file attachment by double-clicking it in your library (see also "Viewing attachments and looking up items" below). Notes automatically display in the right column when you select them.

To create a new attachment, select a citation in your library. Click the New Child Attachment button, which looks like a paper clip. From here you can attach a snapshot of the current page, a link to the current page, a stored copy of a file, or a link to a file. We'll look at each of these cases.

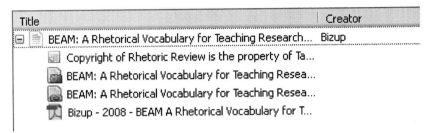

Title	Creator
⊟ 🗋 BEAM: A Rhetorical Vocabulary for Teaching Research... Bizup	
🖼 Copyright of Rhetoric Review is the property of Ta...	
📇 BEAM: A Rhetorical Vocabulary for Teaching Resea...	
📇 BEAM: A Rhetorical Vocabulary for Teaching Resea...	
📕 Bizup - 2008 - BEAM A Rhetorical Vocabulary for T...	

Figure 13.11. This reference has four attachments: a note, a snapshot, a link, and a PDF.

Snapshots

A "snapshot" is a copy of a single web page saved to your library as an item. It includes all the text and images from the page, captured exactly as it exists at the moment you create the snapshot. This is handy for archiving web pages, to keep a record of them in case they disappear later, for offline access, to create a searchable database of a set of pages, or to add your own notes and highlighting to a page.

Snapshots are a duplicate of the currently viewed page, saved to your library on your local computer. Like all attachments, they will synchronize with your online library and use some of your storage quota (see chapter 5). Zotero does its best to preserve the site's original formatting. The results are usually good but not always perfect.

When you save a citation from a web page (see "Saving citations: web pages" above), Zotero automatically creates a snapshot of the page and attaches it to the citation. You can also attach a snapshot to any existing citation by:

- browsing to the page you want to capture,
- selecting a citation in your library,
- clicking the paper clip ("New Child Attachment") menu button above the center column,
- and choosing "Attach Snapshot of Current Page" from the menu.

Zotero will save a snapshot copy of the page and attach it to the selected citation. (You can also make a snapshot of a single image on a page by right-clicking it, choosing Zotero from the popup menu, and then clicking Save Image As Zotero Item.)

Once saved, you can add annotations and highlights to a snapshot file. Open a snapshot by selecting it and clicking View Snapshot in the right column. The snapshot opens in your browser. You can tell at a glance that this is a Zotero attachment and not a page loaded from the web by its address, which consists of "zotero://attachment/" plus a number, instead of a normal http:// address.

Figure 3.12. Use the annotate and highlight buttons at top left to mark up snapshots.

At the top of the page are four buttons (figure 3.12). The first two are used for annotations, small notes within the page. Click the Create Annotation button, the small white speech bubble with the green plus sign. A blank yellow note, like a Post-It, appears on the page wherever you click next. Click on the note and type as much text as you want. Resize the annotation by dragging the right corner. Collapse (hide) it to a small icon by clicking the button in its upper right corner, and display it again by clicking the icon. Move it around the page by clicking the arrow next to the collapse button and moving the mouse, then click again to place it. Delete the annotation by clicking the button in its top left corner. The button next to the Create Annotation button, two white speech bubbles, will collapse or display all the annotations on the snapshot.

Add highlighting to the snapshot by clicking the third button at the top of the page, the yellow highlighter icon. This button toggles highlighting on: any text you select will be highlighted in yellow until you toggle the button off again. The fourth button toggles "unhighlight-ing" on: while active, it removes highlighting from any text you select.

Web Links

A link to a page can also be saved as an attachment, without creating a snapshot. To attach a simple web link to any citation: select the citation, click the Create New Child Attachment menu (the paper clip button), and choose Attach Link to Current Page. Zotero will create a link attachment, which consists only of a title, URL, and dates of access and last modification, plus a space to add text notes. Zotero sometimes adds link attachments to citations automatically (for example, citations saved from Amazon.com always include a link attachment).

Stored Files

To save a file into your library, simply drag it from a folder on your computer into your Zotero pane and release it. This copies the file into the library leaving the original where it is. Drop it on top of a citation to attach it, or into a collection or between items to create an independent or standalone item.

You can set the preferences so that Zotero will automatically save article PDFs along with citations when available. Click the gear menu and choose Preferences, and make sure "Automatically attach associated PDFs and other files when saving items" is checked. When this feature is set, Zotero will attempt to download the PDF copy of an article and save it as an attachment whenever you save a citation.

Two important notes about this feature: first, it only works with a few research sites (at least, it does not with most of the ones I use regularly). For example, it works well with JSTOR but not the EBSCO databases. Your mileage will vary depending on which sites you use for most of your research.

Second, remember that attachments do take up disk space. Stored files will sync with your library, and will take up storage space in your server quota (see chapter 5).

Your attachments are saved in subdirectories of your Zotero directory, either within your Firefox profile folder or in the program directory of the standalone Zotero client. Right-click any stored attachment in the library to get a pop-up menu. Among the other choices, you'll see View, which opens the file in your web browser (if a PDF or HTML file) or in the appropriate application (for example, a PPT file opens in PowerPoint). The Show File menu choice opens the folder on your hard drive that contains the attachment.

Article PDFs saved from databases often have cryptic filenames. To easily give an attached file a human-readable filename, right-click it and choose "Rename File from Parent Metadata." This renames the file according to its parent attachment: for example, from "ELI7041. pdf" to "Educause–2008-7 Things You Should Know About Zotero. pdf". This is an easy way to give your attachments filenames you can recognize at a glance.

Indexing PDF Attachments

Zotero can search the full text of PDFs in your library if you install an optional component. This is very easy and only takes a couple of clicks. Open your Zotero preferences from the gear/action menu and choose the Search tab.

In the section labeled PDF Indexing, click the Check for Installer button (figure 3.13). Within a few seconds, a confirmation window will appear asking whether you wish to install the PDF indexing components. Click Install and wait for the components to download. This may take a few minutes, but you can minimize the window and ignore it while it sets up.

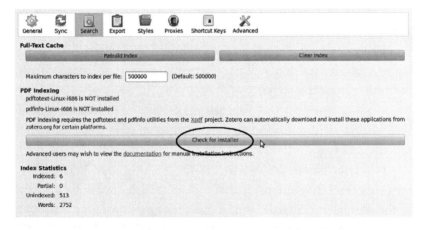

Figure 3.13. To make PDFs searchable in Zotero, click the Search tab on the Preferences screen and click Check for Installer.

Once installed, you can "index" any PDF in your library to make it searchable. Select a PDF attachment in your library. In the right column details you'll see a line labeled "Indexed: No." Click the button with two green arrows next to the "No" to index the file. Zotero "reads" the PDF briefly to make its text searchable and changes the "no" to "yes." You can also index a PDF by right-clicking it in your library and choosing "reindex file" from the menu.

Of course, PDFs must contain text to be indexed. A PDF that contains only images cannot be indexed or made searchable.

File Links

A file link is an attachment that consists of only a link—a pointer—to a file. In other words, the attachment just refers to a file elsewhere on your computer instead of copying it into your library. The advantage of a link is that it takes up no space in your library, but the disadvantage is that if you access your library from a different computer, linked attachments are unavailable. Create a file link by selecting a citation and choosing "Attach link to file."

Notes

A note is a library item that consists solely of text. Notes may be either standalone items or attached to citations. Create notes in several different ways:

- Click the yellow note button at the top center of the Zotero pane and choose "Add standalone note" or (if a citation is selected) "Add child note."
- Select the Notes tab in the right column while viewing an item, and click "Add."
- Zotero often automatically creates notes when saving items from online sources. If an online citation contains information that doesn't fit into any of Zotero's fields, Zotero will sometimes save the "extra" information into an attached note.

To edit the contents of a note, just type in the text window (figure 3.14). Use the toolbar above the text window to format your text (add bold, italics, and so on) if needed. Double-click any note in your library to open it in a new and larger window that can be resized if needed.

The contents of all notes in your library are searchable.

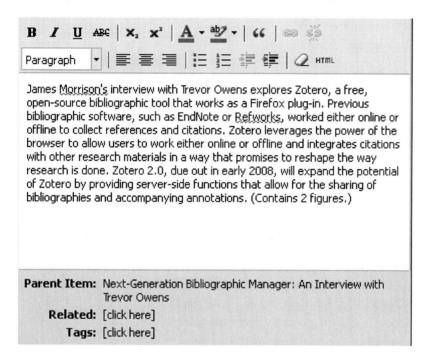

Figure 3.14. The note editor. It's similar to text editors in many other programs.

Viewing Attachments And Looking Up Items

To the right of the search box there's a green arrow, the Locate button. This allows you to view attachments, or look up any citation in your university's library or in other search tools like Google Scholar.

Select any reference in your library and click the Locate button. The dropdown list (figure 3.15) gives you a choice of tools to use to view this item. If the item includes a URL, or has PDFs or other attachments, the first choices on the menu may include:

- View PDF/View Snapshot: open the PDF or snapshot attachment in a browser window

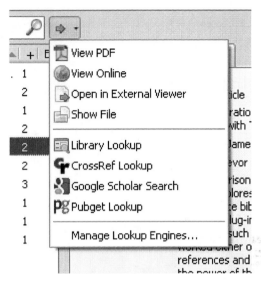

Figure 3.15: The Locate menu provides options for viewing attachments and URLs and for looking up references online.

- View Online: open the associated URL in a browser
- Open in External Viewer: open the attachment in another program (usually Adobe Reader for PDFs, but other types of files will open in the appropriate application)
- Show File: open the folder on your hard drive (inside your Zotero directory) that contains the attachment file

The above choices change depending on what types of attachments the reference has.

The Locate button also allows you to look up books and articles in a library's catalog or database. Choosing Library Lookup from the menu searches for the item (book or article) online. By default, Library Lookup uses the open WorldCat catalog to search for items. You can specify your own university's library, however:

- Click gear menu/Preferences and choose Advanced (figure 3.16).
- At the bottom of this window is an "OpenURL" section. OpenURL is a library server that searches the library's catalog and online journals.

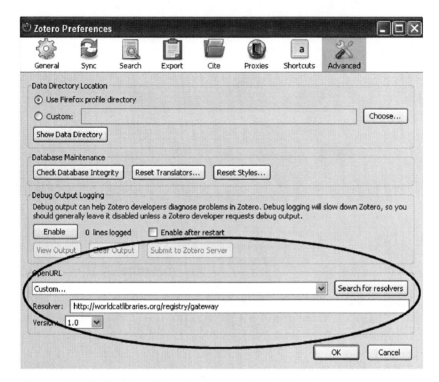

Figure 3.16. Use the "Search for resolvers " button or enter your library's OpenURL address in the Advanced tab of Preferences.

- If you're on campus, click "Search for resolvers" and Zotero may be able to find your library's server automatically. Choose your institution from the drop-down menu.
- If you're not on campus, check with your reference desk or web/systems librarian to see if they can provide you with your OpenURL address.

Once this preference has been set, Library Lookup will check your own university's library holdings to locate the item you've selected. It should open in a new window with links to your catalog or online databases.

Other search tools available from the Locate menu include Google Scholar, CrossRef (for looking up items with Digital Object Identifier [DOI] numbers), and the Pubget article search engine. Choose which searches appear on this menu by choosing Manage Lookup Engines from the Locate menu.

Searching Your Library

Of course, one of the main advantages to saving all your research materials into a library is so that you can find them again easily.

Basic Search

Simply start typing a word or name into the search box at the top of the center column. As you type, the center column will display all matches from the currently viewed library or collection.

The basic search shows matches from everything in your library: author names, titles, subjects, tags, and the contents of notes and indexed attachments. (When searching a large library or collection, this can sometimes be slow because Zotero searches each character as you type it. To speed up the search, put quotation marks around your search. Zotero will not search for each letter individually but will wait until you close the quotation marks.)

Remember that PDFs are not searchable unless you index them: see "Indexing PDF attachments" above.

Advanced Search

For a more precise search, click the magnifying glass to the left of the search box. This opens the advanced search window. Don't let the name scare you: as in most search tools, "advanced" just means it provides more options.

The most common use of the advanced search is to search one or more fields specifically: just to search author names or titles, for example. The first search box defaults to a title search, which you can change by clicking Title to bring up a drop-down menu. You can specify a search of any field, and search multiple fields at once by clicking the plus sign at the right of the screen to add more search boxes.

Use the middle drop-down list to choose the type of match: "contains" matches any part of the field, "is" requires an exact match, and "does not contain" and "is not" do the opposite, of course, excluding anything that matches the text you enter.

Checkboxes below the search boxes allow you to search subfolders of a collection, limit your search to only top-level items (that is, excluding attachments), or to show both parent and child items.

The percent sign (%) is a "wildcard" character that will match any characters in a search. For example, searching for "environment%" will match environment, environmental, environmentalists, and anything else that starts with "environment." "s%d" would find "sad," "started," "solid" and anything else that starts with S and ends with D, no matter how many characters in between.

Saved Searches in Use

Kate has asked her grad student assistant Anita to track down all the sources listed in a published literature review. While she works on this project, Anita has to keep track of which sources the library has, which she has already obtained and which ones she needs to request via interlibrary loan.

Anita first searches for all the citations online and saves them to her Zotero library. She adds a custom tag to all the citations: "#needed" (she decides to add a hashmark to her custom tags for her own convenience, just to visually distinguish them). Then she sets up a saved search for "Tag is #needed".

She adds additional tags as she works: #library for articles her university library has, #requested for the ones she requests via ILL, and changes #needed or #requested to #obtained for the ones she has actually gotten her hands on. She sets up saved searches for each tag so she can keep track of the status of each item. Over the next few days, she updates tags as she works and her citations move from the #needed list to #library or #requested as she tracks them down, until they are all in the #obtained list and ready to give to Kate.[4]

Saved Searches

From the advanced search screen you can also save a search to your library. Saving a search makes a new list of all matches to your search, and automatically updates that list as new matching items are added to your collection. Click Save Search on the advanced search screen to create a new saved search. Saved searches appear in the left column below your collections (the icon for a saved search is a folder with a magnifying glass).

For example, if I am researching podcasting, I might search for all items in my library that have "podcast%" in the Title or Tag fields. If I save this search, it creates a list of all matching items. From then on, any time I save an item with "podcast" (or "podcasting" or "podcasts") in the title or tags, it automatically appears in the saved search list.

Deleting and Undeleting Items

To delete an item from your library, right-click it and choose "Delete Selected Item From Library." To remove it from a collection you're currently viewing but not delete it altogether, right-click the item and click "Remove Selected Item" ("...from this collection" is implicit).

The Delete key is a shortcut: when viewing a collection, pressing delete removes the selected item from the collection but not the library. When viewing My Library, pressing delete removes the item from the library entirely and moves it to the Trash.

All deleted items go into the Trash folder, located below your library and below all of your collections. The Trash works like the trash or recycle bin on your desktop. Items stay in the Trash until you empty them. If you change your mind about deleting an item, just drag it from the Trash back into your library. Empty the Trash by right-clicking it and choosing Empty Trash from the menu. Your Trash folder does synchronize with your library online, and attachments in the Trash do take up quota space (see chapter 5).

Saving a Copy of your Library

You may want to save your library (or just one collection or specific items) in order to give a copy to someone, to have it available on a flash drive, move it to another computer or just to have a backup copy. (Synchronizing your library, chapter 5, does keep an automatic backup for you, but you might want a redundant copy.)

Exporting a copy of anything in your library is easy. Select either My Library, a collection, or individual items and right-click. Choose

"Export" from the pop-up menu. If you'll be using the exported items in Zotero, choose "Zotero RDF" from the drop-down list. (Selecting "Export Notes" and/or "Export Files" will include notes and/or attachments.) If you'll be using the items with another program, you probably want to export in RIS format (see "Moving to (and from) Zotero" below).

Click OK and save. Exporting to Zotero RDF creates a folder containing an .RDF file. To import this file into Zotero on another computer, select "Import" from the gear menu and browse to that .RDF file.

Moving to (and from) Zotero

Experienced researchers who use other reference managers like End-Note, Mendeley or RefWorks often ask about moving their personal library from their former software of choice into Zotero. This is usually easy, with a few caveats. The same is true for transferring citation data from Zotero to another program, for example to share citations with a colleague using EndNote.

Since Zotero is built on open standards, it can import and export references in a number of file formats that are common to most bibliographic software. This gives the two programs a "common language" to read each others' data.

Zotero can import any of the following formats:
- Bibliontology RDF
- MODS (Metadata Object Description Schema)
- BibTeX
- RIS
- Refer/BibIX
- RDF
- CTX
- MAB2
- MARC

...but don't worry if these acronyms don't mean anything to you. The most commonly used file format among bibliographic software is RIS. Most users can ignore the other formats unless they have a specific need for them.

Nearly all reference manager software can read and write a format called RIS (which stands for Research Information Systems, the former publisher of a bibliographic program called Reference Manager now made by Thomson Reuters). This makes it a useful common format for reference managers; in fact many online databases use the RIS format for downloading citation data since it is so widely used.

The general steps to transfer citations from another program into Zotero are:

- Use the other program's Export feature to save your library into RIS format. The details of this step vary from program to program, of course. In EndNote, click the File menu and click Export. In RefWorks, click References and then Export.
- You should have a choice of file format to export. Look for a choice labeled RIS, RefMan, or Reference Manager. Save the file.
- This generally creates a file with a .TXT or .RIS extension. (The RIS format is just a text file containing citations formatted in a standard way. You can open it with a text editor if you're curious about what the contents look like.)
- Open Zotero. Click the gear/action menu and choose Import, and simply browse to the RIS file you just saved. When you open that file, Zotero will import your citations into your library in a new collection labeled with the current date and time.

Important note: Exporting a RIS file into Zotero will not import PDFs and other attachments—just the citations and metadata! Users with a large library of PDFs may want to try the "Retrieve metadata for PDF" feature (see "Indexing PDF attachments" above).[5]

Several libraries have created excellent step-by-step guides to importing and exporting between the reference managers they support.[6,7] The audience for such a guide might also be interested in information like feature comparisons or other ways in which different programs can interact, such as Zotero's ability to import EndNote bibliographic styles.

Notes

1. Center for History and New Media, "proxies [Zotero Documentation]."
2. Unfortunately for legal researchers, at this writing neither Lexis-Nexis nor Westlaw work with Zotero. Hein Online, however, does, and the latest version of the Bluebook style was written by an attorney.
3. If you have both EndNote and Zotero installed on your computer, Zotero will usually "take over" and import any exported citations, preventing them from going to EndNote. You can disable the Zotero add-on and restart the browser to allow EndNote to receive exported citations. Re-enable the add-on to use Zotero again.
4. Mullen, "How to Create a Work Flow in Zotero."
5. In some cases it may be possible to transfer a large EndNote library with PDFs by using scripts to rewrite the RIS file, but this may be more trouble than many users want to take. See Center for History and New Media, "kb:importing_records_from_endnote [Zotero Documentation]."
6. George Mason University Libraries, "Citation Migration."
7. Princeton University Library, "Export to RW/EN/Zotero."

Further Reading

Center for History and New Media. "Attaching files." *Zotero*, 2010. http://www.zotero.org/support/attaching_files.

———. "Getting stuff into your library." *Zotero*, 2010. http://www.zotero.org/support/getting_stuff_into_your_library.

———. "Zotero—Quick Start Guide", 2009. http://www.zotero.org/documentation/quick_start_guide.

———. "kb:importing_records_from_endnote [Zotero Documentation]." *Zotero*, 2009. http://www.zotero.org/support/kb/importing_records_from_endnote.

———. "proxies [Zotero Documentation]." *Zotero*, 2010. http://www.zotero.org/support/proxies.

Clark, Brian, and John Stierman. "Identify, Organize, and Retrieve Items Using Zotero." *Teacher Librarian* 37, no. 2 (December 1, 2009): 54–56,.

George Mason University Libraries. "Citation Migration", 2008. http://citationmigration.gmu.edu/.

Morrison, James L., and Trevor Owens. "Next-Generation Bibliographic Manager: An Interview with Trevor Owens." *Innovate: Journal of Online Education* 4, no. 2 (2008). http://www.innovateonline.info/index.php?view=article&id=540.

Mullen, Lincoln. "How to Create a Work Flow in Zotero." *Backward Glance*, August 28, 2009. http://lincolnmullen.com/2009/08/28/how-to-create-a-work-flow-in-zotero/.

Princeton University Library. "Export to RW/EN/Zotero." *Using RefWorks at Princeton*, 2011. http://libguides.princeton.edu/content.php?pid=30227&sid=230429.

Puckett, Jason. "Zotero [GSU Library guide]", 2010. http://research.library.gsu.edu/zotero.

CHAPTER 4 Creating Bibliographies and Writing with Zotero

The previous chapter covered putting "stuff" into Zotero: saving citations, attaching files, and organizing and searching what you've put into your library. This chapter covers the reverse situation: once the references are saved to the library, using them to produce bibliographies and other forms of output.

Zotero can produce bibliographies in two basic ways. First, you can easily make a bibliography by simply selecting items from the library, choosing a style, and saving or pasting them to a file. This method allows you to create bibliographies that can go into any type of file: documents, text files, web pages, Google Docs or anywhere else. One advantage to creating bibliographies in this way is that they contain the data needed for Zotero to save citations: that is, if a Zotero bibliography is posted to the web, anyone else can save the citations from that bibliography.

The second method of building bibliographies requires the word processor toolbars mentioned briefly in chapter 2. The toolbars for Microsoft Word, OpenOffice and NeoOffice allow writers to insert in-text citations or footnotes from a Zotero library into the document and build the bibliography automatically as new citations are added. In other words, each time you cite a source in your text, Zotero adds that citation to the bibliography in the correct order.

Zotero includes fifteen different bibliographic styles when first installed, including MLA, APA, Turabian and four variants of Chicago style, which probably covers the needs of most writers. Approximately 1400 additional styles are available for download from zotero.org/styles.

Quick and Easy Bibliographies

Creating a bibliography from the library is simple and can be done in just a couple of clicks. Bibliographies created in this way can be inserted into any document or text file.

The two ways of creating quick bibliographies (which I call "click and paste" and "drag and drop") are useful for creating simple bibliographies for short papers, or bibliographies to go into a web page. For longer writing projects, the "Zotero and Word Processors" section below may be more useful: it outlines how to create in-text citations and footnotes, and bibliographies that automatically update themselves as citations are added to the document.

Use one of the following two methods when you need to create an annotated bibliography, since they simply create citations as regular text in the document to which you can add your own annotations.

Click and Paste

This is perhaps the most basic way to create a bibliography with Zotero. Just select the citations, choose the style, and paste the bibliography into your document (or save or print it).

First, select the references in the library. Either select individual items from the center column, select everything in the center column with control-A/command-A, or select a collection in the left column. Right-click your selected items and choose Create Bibliography.

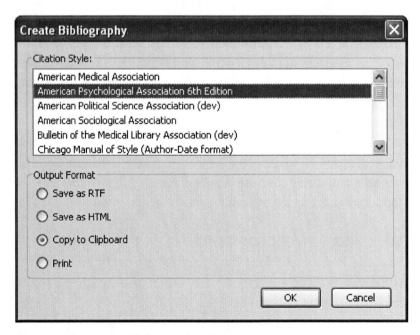

Figure 4.1. Create Bibliography dialog

Next, select the style you want. Zotero remembers the last style you used and will select it by default. (If you need a style not in this list, see the "Bibliographic Styles" section below for instructions on downloading more styles.)

Finally, choose "Copy to clipboard," click OK, and simply paste it into your document. The bibliography will appear in the style you chose. This is a good moment to check it for accuracy! If you notice any mistakes in the citations, it is a good idea to correct them in the Zotero library itself so that the reference will be accurate for future bibliographies.

Using Zotero Bibliographies on the Web

Nathan is creating a research guide on the web for an undergraduate journalism class. He's including some citations to some recommended books. He creates a Zotero collection for the class, saves the citations from the library catalog, right-clicks the collection and saves it as an HTML file. He adds that bit of HTML code to his web page and sends Kate, the professor, the URL to share with her class.

Ian opens the research guide on his laptop at home. He notices that Zotero shows a folder icon, clicks it, and is presented with a list of references to save. He selects them all and saves them to *his* Zotero collection for the class.

When you choose Create Bibliography, notice that there are options besides copying and pasting. Under Output Format, there are also choices to save to RTF, save to HTML and print.

Save your bibliography to Rich Text Format (RTF) if you want to create it as a file for use in a word processor. RTF is a standard format that all word processors on any operating system can read. It retains formatting like bold, italics and underlining. Double-clicking an RTF file on most computers opens it in Word or OpenOffice.

Zotero can also save bibliographies to HTML for use on the web. This includes all the markup tags needed to preserve the correct formatting. It also includes all the citation metadata—the code that Zotero needs to *save* an item from the web. In other words, when a bibliography created by Zotero is viewed in a web browser, the browser displays capture icons in the address bar so that the reader can save those same citations to her own library.

The final choice, below Copy to Clipboard, is Print. No surprises here: this opens a standard print dialog box.

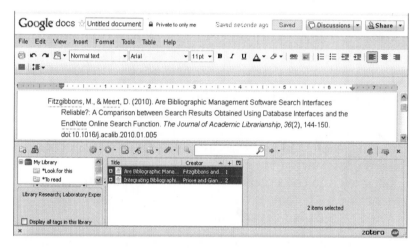

Figure 4.2. Drag and drop references from Zotero to Google Docs to create a bibliography in the default style.

Drag and Drop and Default Styles

Perhaps even simpler, you can literally drag references from the Zotero library into any text field in your web browser. This is particularly useful when writing in Google Docs (figure 4.2).

The citations will appear fully formatted in the default style. To set your default style, open Zotero's preferences window (from the gear menu), click the Export tab (the clipboard icon), and choose the style you use most from the drop-down menu. All drag-and-drop bibliographies will be formatted in this style. (Keyboard shortcut: control-alt-C copies selected references to the clipboard in the default style, for pasting anywhere.)

The default style can be customized on a per-site basis, so that drag-and-drop bibliographies appear in different styles on different sites.

On the same Export preferences window, click the + button below the Site-Specific Settings window, type in part of a URL and choose the style from the Output Format menu.

For example, if you usually use Chicago style but need to use APA on a PBworks site you're building, set your default style to Chicago, click the + under Site-Specific Settings, type pbworks.com as the domain and choose APA under Output Format for that site. Any references you drag into a pbworks.com page will be formatted in APA, and any you drag into other sites (like Google Docs) will be in Chicago style.

Zotero and Google Docs

The click-and-paste or drag-and-drop methods are the best ways (the only ways, really) to use Zotero with the online Google Docs word processor. There is no way to install a Zotero toolbar into Google Docs since it exists only on the web.

I do a great deal of my writing, at least first drafts, in Google Docs. It's convenient since all of my documents are accessible from any computer. Creating drag-and-drop bibliographies from Zotero is easy (both tools are in the browser window if I'm using Firefox) and works well. When using Zotero with Docs, remember to set the preferences to reflect your desired bibliographic style.

Using Google Docs with Zotero carries a few disadvantages. Zotero has no way to interact directly with Docs the way it can with Word or OpenOffice. This means that there is no way for Zotero to create in-text citations in a Docs document, nor can it create bibliographies that update automatically as you write.

RTF Scan

If you add citations within a document file in a special way, Zotero can scan the document, add citations and format the bibliography when you're done writing. This feature is called "RTF Scan." It's not as intuitive or easy as using the word processor toolbars (see the next section of this chapter), but it doesn't require installing any additional plugins besides Zotero itself.

Type in-text citations within curly braces as you write: for example, "{Puckett, 2010}." See the list at right for the citation formats that will work.[1] Type "{Bibliography}" wherever you want the bibliography to appear, or leave it out to have the bibliography automatically placed at the end of the document.

When finished, use your word processor's "Save As" function to save the document as an RTF file. RTF stands for Rich Text Format; it's a universal format that any word processor can read and write.

Formatting Citations for RTF Scan

The RTF Scan feature can read citations typed in any of these formats:
{Smith, 2009}
Smith {2009}
{Smith et al., 2009}
{John Smith, 2009}
{Smith, 2009, 10–14}
{Smith, "Title", 2009}
{Jones, 2005; Smith, 2009}

Now open Zotero. Click the gear menu and choose "RTF Scan." Next to "Input File," click Choose File and browse to the RTF document you just saved. "Output File" will default to the name of your input document with "(Scanned)" appended to the end of the filename, but you can of course give it a different name or location by clicking Choose File and selecting a new destination. Click Next when ready to proceed.

Zotero now attempts to match (or "map") your bracketed citations in the document to references in your library. The next screen lets you verify the citations before creating the finished document. Zotero displays three categories: unmapped citations, ambiguous citations, and mapped citations.

Unmapped citations are those for which Zotero was unable to find a match. Click the icon to the right of an unmapped citation to browse the library yourself and choose the correct reference.

Ambiguous citations match more than one reference in your library. Possible matches show below each ambiguous citation—click the icon with the green arrow to choose the correct reference, or click the icon to the right of the ambiguous citation to browse the library for the correct one.

Citations for which Zotero did find a match are shown as mapped citations at the bottom of the window. Click the icon to the right of a mapped citation to change the reference.

When you have chosen references for all ambiguous and unmapped citations, click Next. Choose the desired bibliographic style on the next screen and then click Finish. Open the output file and don't forget to check the finished product for accuracy.

Zotero and Word Processors
Installing the Toolbar

The methods above don't require any software other than Zotero itself to create bibliographies. By installing the appropriate toolbar, though, a word processor can pull citations from the library, format the in-text citations or footnotes in the document, and automatically build a bibliography as the user writes. Zotero toolbars are available for Word for Windows, Word for MacOS, and OpenOffice (or NeoOffice) for Windows, MacOS or Linux. Standalone Zotero includes these toolbars; you'll only need to install them separately if you are using Zotero for Firefox.

Quick Instructions: Installing the Word Processor Toolbars

1. Close your word processor.
2. Go to zotero.org/support/word_processor_plugin_installation in Firefox. (If several versions of Zotero are listed, follow the instructions on the page and choose the version you're using.)
   a) Windows Word users, click **Install Word for Windows Plugin**
   b) Mac Word users, click **Install PythonExt**, install as in step 3, then click Install Word for Mac Plugin.
   c) OpenOffice users (any OS), click Install **OpenOffice Plugin**.
3. Click Allow, then Install.
4. Wait for the plugin to download, restart Firefox.
5. Open your word processor.

If you didn't install the word processor toolbar when you installed Zotero, you can add it at any time. Open Zotero.org in Firefox and click the "Download word processor plugins" link (zotero.org/support/word_processor_plugin_installation). Close your word processor before you start.

Choose your word processor from the list on this page. (There may be multiple versions of Zotero listed; choose the word processor plugin that matches your version of Zotero.) Most people probably use Word for Windows, so it appears first. (Most of my examples feature Word for Windows.) For **Word for Windows and OpenOffice**, just click "Install the Word for Windows Plugin" or "Install the OpenOffice Plugin." The installation process is exactly like installing Zotero or any other Firefox plugin: Click Allow, then Install, then restart Firefox.

Mac Word users, note the two steps spelled out in the instructions on the installation page. First, click "install PythonExt from zotero.org"—this is a software component required by the Zotero plugin. It takes a little longer to download than Zotero, so don't worry. Then install the Word plugin from the "Install the Word for Mac Plugin" link. For both components, the procedure is the same: Click Allow, then Install, then restart Firefox.

Open the word processor and locate the Zotero toolbar:

- In Word for Windows version 2007 or later, click the Add-Ins tab. The toolbar appears here, probably the only one visible (figure 4.3).
- In Word 2008 for Mac, Zotero uses a menu instead of a toolbar (figure 4.4). Click the Script menu (the small icon to the right of Help). All the functions are the same, but Mac users will need to mentally translate some instructions from "click this button on the toolbar" into "click this item in the Script/Zotero menu." Older versions of Word for Mac use the standard toolbar.

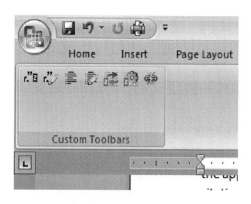

Figure 4.3. Zotero toolbar in Word for Windows, under the Add-Ins menu tab.

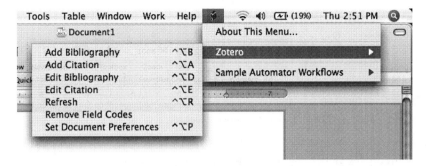

Figure 4.4. The Zotero menu in Word for MacOS, located under the script menu next to Help.

- In OpenOffice Writer, the toolbar appears along with all the other icons below the menu (figure 4.5). If it isn't obviously visible, look for the row of reddish buttons; the first one on the toolbar looks like a lowercase R, a quotation mark and a small red Z. (The Word and OpenOffice toolbars look the same.)

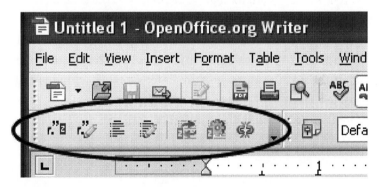

Figure 4.5. The Zotero toolbar in OpenOffice Writer.

Since Zotero releases frequent updates and new versions, there may be multiple versions of the word processor toolbar on the installation page. Each version of Zotero must use its corresponding version of the toolbar—this will be clearly indicated on the Zotero site.

Fixing the Toolbar

Rarely, the toolbar will be installed correctly but won't appear in the word processor. This can usually be fixed by taking the following steps:

- Close the word processor.
- Open Zotero's preferences (gear menu/Preferences).
- Click the Cite tab, the Word Processors sub-tab and then the "Reinstall Word Add-in" (or "Reinstall OpenOffice Extension") button.
- Restart Firefox or your word processor if prompted.

This quick process fixes most toolbar problems. For help with other word processor toolbar problems, see the suggestions on the Zotero site.[2]

Using the Word/OpenOffice Toolbar

The Word (or OpenOffice) toolbar creates a connection between the word processor and the Zotero library. It allows the writer to "pull" references from her library, creates in-text citations or footnotes in the document, automatically formats them in the desired style, and builds the bibliography as the writer adds new citations. (The toolbar works the same for Microsoft Word and OpenOffice Writer, so for brevity's sake I will refer to it as the "Word toolbar" hereafter, with the understanding that all of these instructions apply to OpenOffice users as well.)

Important note: Word has a built-in citation management feature called References. When using Zotero, remember that you're using it *instead* of the Word feature. Use the Zotero toolbar and ignore the References tab in the Word menu bar entirely.

The toolbar has seven buttons. In order, they are:

- Insert Citation: This button adds in-text citations or footnotes to the document. Citations appear at the cursor's location when you click Insert Citation.
- Edit Citation: This allows the writer to change an existing citation: add or edit page numbers, for example, or change the citation to an entirely different source.
- Insert Bibliography: This adds the automatically generated bibliography to the document at the cursor's location (usually at the end, but it can go anywhere in the document).
- Edit Bibliography: This button allows the writer to add references to customize the bibliography as needed, and to edit individual references.

- Refresh: Clicking this button "re-reads" all references in the document, updating them to show any changes made in the Zotero library.
- Doc Prefs (short for document preferences): This button is used to change bibliographic styles, but can also make changes in how the references are stored within the document.
- Remove Codes: This removes all special Zotero code from the document.

Quick Reference: Inserting a Citation

1. Click the Insert Citation button on the Zotero toolbar in Word.
2. When you insert the first citation, choose a bibliographic style from the list and click OK.
3. Browse or search to choose the reference you want to cite. Optionally enter a page number.
4. Click OK.

Citing Sources

Start writing just as you normally would. When you reach a point in the document where you'd type an in-text citation or a footnote, click the first button on the Zotero toolbar, Insert Citation (Mac Word users: click "Add Citation" from the Zotero menu). Zotero must be running in order to cite sources from your library.

The first time you cite a source in a document, Zotero presents a list of all the bibliographic styles available. Scroll through the list, click the desired style, and click OK. This indicates to Zotero what style this document should use. You can bring back this dialog box and choose a new style at any time by clicking the Doc Prefs button.

(Two other options appear on this dialog box: First, some styles offer a choice between footnotes and endnotes. This choice will be grayed out if it doesn't apply to the selected style. Second, some styles offer a choice between "Fields" or "ReferenceMarks" and "Bookmarks." This affects how the word processor saves the citation information in terms of its internal data format. If a document is to be shared between Word and OpenOffice, choose Bookmarks. Most users can leave this set to the default of Fields or ReferenceMarks and ignore it.)

Once the style is set, a window opens displaying the Zotero library. This gives full browsing access to the entire library, including all collections and group libraries, plus a small search box at the top. Browse or search for the reference you wish to cite and select it. If you need to cite a page number for this source, type it in the Page box at the bottom right. (The Page box can be used to cite other parts of a source; change the drop-down menu to change "page" to "figure" or "chapter," for example.) The Prefix and Suffix boxes will add text to the beginning or end of a citation (such as "see also"). Click OK to insert the citation into the document.

Select the Suppress Author checkbox to leave the author name out of the citation. This is useful when you name the author in your text—for example, "Smith's study shows … (2008, p. 22)"—and don't need to include it again in the in-text citation.

CITING MULTIPLE SOURCES

To cite more than one reference in a single citation, click the Insert Citation button as usual, and then click the Multiple Sources button. A new pane appears at the right of the Insert Citation window, with four arrow buttons (up, down, left and right) next to it. The new right-hand pane shows the references you will be citing. Use the arrow buttons to choose and order the references in your citation.

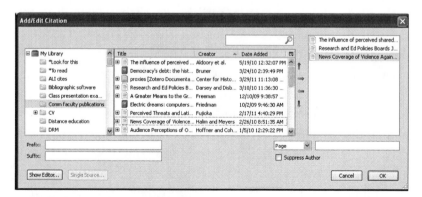

Figure 4.6. Cite multiple references at once

Browse your library in the left and middle columns, and choose the references to cite with the right arrow button (think of it as moving the citation from the library rightwards into the citation pane). To remove a reference from the citation, use the left button (pointing from the citation pane back into the library). Use the up and down arrow buttons to choose the order of citations by moving them up and down. Add page numbers to each reference the same way as usual, by selecting the reference and typing in the Page box. Click OK to add the citation to the document.

This sounds more complicated on paper than it really is. Try it once and you will probably find it quite intuitive: right arrow adds references, left removes them, and up and down change the order. Otherwise, citing multiple references works exactly the same as citing single ones.

EDITING CITATIONS

Editing a citation, such as adding or changing a page number, suppressing an author name, or even changing which source to cite, is easy. Click the citation in your document and click the second button on the Word toolbar, Edit Citation. (In Windows and Linux it looks just like the Insert Citation button with a yellow pencil in place of the red Z.)

Clicking Edit Citation opens the same dialog as inserting a citation, with all the same options. You can change any element of the citation, including citing an entirely different source. Click OK to update the citation in your document.

Adding Bibliographies

So far we've added citations to the text, but the document still lacks a bibliography.

Place the cursor at the end of the document (or wherever you want the bibliography to appear) and click the third button on the toolbar, Insert Bibliography. It looks like a series of horizontal red lines and is meant to resemble a tiny list of references. (Mac Word users: click "Add bibliography" from the Zotero menu.)

The bibliography appears wherever your cursor is located in the document, consisting of all the sources you have cited so far. As you cite more sources, they appear in the bibliography in the correct order: either alphabetical or in the order cited, depending on which bibliographic style you chose when you cited your first source.

EDITING BIBLIOGRAPHIES

Click the Edit Bibliography button, the fourth button on the toolbar. (In keeping with the theme of the other buttons, this one looks like the Insert Bibliography button with a yellow pencil added.)

The Edit Bibliography window allows you to add or remove references to or from the bibliography. Use the left and right arrows to add or remove references. They work in the same way as citing multiple sources: right arrow adds a reference to the bibliography, left arrow removes it.

If you have cited a source in the text but for some reason want to omit it from the bibliography, select it in the right pane and click the left arrow. To include a source in the bibliography that you have not cited in the document, browse the library in the left and middle panes, select the desired reference and move it into the bibliography by clicking the right arrow.

The Edit Bibliography window also provides a way to make changes to the final citation. Select any reference in the right column (below "References in Bibliography"). Its citation appears in the bottom of the Edit Bibliography window. This citation can be edited manually by adding or deleting text, or by reformatting using the bold, italic, underline and super- and subscript buttons.

Use this feature cautiously: the citation will retain any changes you make here, but will no longer update based on changes you make to your Zotero library or to the document style. In other words, if you correct an error in your Zotero library or change bibliographic styles the manually edited citation will not update.

You can remove your manual changes with the Revert button at the bottom left of the window. Revert All resets all references in the bibliography to the version automatically created by Zotero.

Multiple Bibliographies

Longer documents like book and thesis manuscripts may require multiple bibliographies, perhaps one for each chapter. There's no way for Zotero to maintain multiple bibliographies in one document if you use the Word toolbar, so you have two options: create multiple documents, or copy and paste multiple bibliographies instead of using the toolbar.

First, you can create a document for each chapter, and use the Word toolbar to create your citations and automatically update your bibliography in each chapter. It's usually convenient to create a collection for each chapter as well. The inconvenience is that you'll have to keep your project in several documents, not just one.

Second, you can keep the project all in one document file and use the copy and paste method to create bibliographies at the end of each chapter. You'll lose the convenience of having Zotero create your citations for you, but only have one document file as your finished product.

Refreshing the Bibliography

The Refresh button (two gray arrows in a circle) causes the word processor to "re-read" all the citation information from the Zotero library and rewrite the bibliography and in-text citations. This is useful, for example, if you have edited a reference in the library and need to update the document to reflect your changes.

Zotero performs this "refresh" process whenever you insert a new citation into the document. The toolbar button just allows you to force a refresh without inserting a citation.

If you have edited any citations or any part of the bibliography in the document itself—that is, by typing citation changes into Word, not by making changes within the Zotero library—refreshing the document will undo all of those changes and re-write all citations and the bibliography based on the contents of the library. In other words, to correct a mistake in a citation, go to the library and fix it there, because Zotero periodically updates the document based on the references in your library. Changes made to the bibliography "by hand" in the document won't stick.

Document Preferences

The Doc Prefs (document preferences) button allows you to change the bibliographic style of a document, or change between Bookmarks/ReferenceMarks and Fields. See "Citing sources" above for more information.

Remove Codes

The last button on the toolbar, Remove Codes, strips the document of all the special code that allows Zotero to edit and update citations and bibliographies. This might be useful if you are having difficulty opening a document containing Zotero citations in an older word processor, for example.

Removing the Zotero code from a document breaks the "link" between the document and Zotero and converts the bibliography and citations to ordinary Word/OpenOffice text that Zotero can no longer edit. Use this feature only if you are finished using Zotero with a document, and consider making a backup copy first.

Annotated Bibliographies

One limitation of Zotero is that in most cases there is no easy way to embed annotations to a citation (as a note, for example) and have them appear automatically in an annotated bibliography.

The simplest solution is to create a bibliography using the copy-and-paste or drag-and-drop method, then simply add annotations by typing them beneath each entry. Annotations could be initially created in the library by adding them as notes, then copied and pasted into the final document one by one. This would preserve them for future projects and make them searchable.

At present there's only one citation style available that creates annotated bibliography: a custom version of Chicago. Historians are in luck: a Zotero user has created a Chicago annotated style available for download from zotero.org/styles (look for the style called "Chicago Manual of Style (Annotated Bibliography)"). Add annotations to the Extra field in the library and they will appear in the bibliography.

Bibliographic Styles

Zotero includes fifteen bibliographic styles when installed: APA, MLA, a few variants of Chicago style, and a handful of others. Hundreds more are available to download (for free, of course) from the Zotero Style Repository at zotero.org/styles.

Installing a new style (or updating an existing one) is easy: open the Style Repository page in Firefox, browse or search the list, and click the Install link next to the desired style. Click the Install button on the confirmation dialog window that opens and the new style will be installed instantly.

One of the drawbacks to Zotero is that it lacks a built-in style editor like EndNote's. Zotero styles are written in a format called Citation Style Language (CSL). There are a number of CSL editors in the works at this writing, but none have reached a state of user-friendly completeness yet.[3] (The Zotero Style Repository is presently the largest library of CSL styles on the web.[4])

If you need a style that isn't included in Zotero, you have a few options.

1. Check the Zotero Style Repository (zotero.org/styles) as noted above. Search the page for the name of the style you need and click Install.

2. Zotero can import a few EndNote styles, which are available to download even if you don't own EndNote. Search the list at endnote.com/support/enstyles.asp and save the .ENS (EndNote Style) file from the Download link. Open Zotero's Preferences from the gear menu. Click the Cite tab, then the Styles tab. Click the plus (+) button below the list of installed styles. Set the file type to "EndNote Styles" and browse to where you saved the .ENS file. CHNM has stated that they're no longer supporting this feature, so don't count on this to work consistently: some EndNote styles import with no problem. Some simply don't seem to work with Zotero.

3. Check the Zotero forums to see if someone else has already requested the style you need. (The Citation Styles forum is at zotero.org/forum/11.) If not, post a request. Make sure you include all the information at zotero.org/support/requesting_styles in your request. The Zotero community includes many volunteers who create custom styles; someone may be able to help!

Journal Abbreviations

Many citation styles in the sciences require abbreviated journal titles. Zotero cannot automatically abbreviate full journal titles, nor can it import lists of titles and abbreviations. It is highly dependent on being able to import accurate information from the research database. Science researchers should check their bibliographies carefully for journal titles' consistency.

Some databases (e.g., Web of Science) only provide Zotero with a full unabbreviated journal title. Some (e.g., PubMed) provide both the full title and abbreviation. If the database provides both, Zotero saves the abbreviated title to the "Journal Abbr" field in the reference.

If the bibliographic style calls for an abbreviated journal title in the citation, Zotero will use the abbreviation. If the Journal Abbreviation field is empty, Zotero uses the full title. Depending on what database you saved the citation from, you may need to add journal abbreviations to the library yourself.

Reports

In addition to standard bibliographies, Zotero can create reports—HTML documents listing all the items in a collection or a group of selected items. A report is simply a list displaying all your references in the browser window, in a format easy to print or save. Reports list all fields in your references: Author, title, dates, pages, everything—and include notes and the titles of any attachments.

To create a report, right-click a collection (or any selected references) and choose "Generate Report." The report displays in your browser window, ready to save, print or copy. No customization is available: reports simply list everything you've selected and do not display in any citation style. (But see jasonpriem.com/projects/report_cleaner.php for a web application that can fine-tune the output of a Zotero report.)

Reports also include information about citations such as the date the reference was added and modified. This can be a useful way for teachers to track students' research progress.[5]

Timelines

The timeline feature gives you a chronological visualization of your library or a collection. A timeline is an interactive scrolling display of your references that allows you to view them chronologically.

To create a timeline, select either your library or a collection in the left column. Click the gear menu button and choose "Create Timeline." A timeline based on your selection appears in the browser window (figure 4.7).

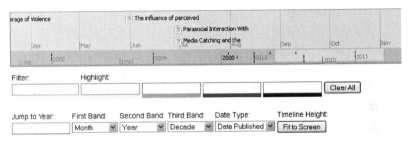

Figure 4.7. Timelines show a visual representation of the dates represented in your library

The timeline is divided into bands. The top light gray band, divided into months, contains your references with appropriate icons indicating books, articles and so on. References appear in chronological order. The medium gray band below that represents years, and the darker gray band at the bottom, decades. Clicking any reference opens it in your Zotero library. Drag the timeline left or right to see newer or older references or use the Jump to Year button to navigate directly to a year.

The default chronology is publication date. Change this to sort by the date the reference was added or modified using the Date Type drop-down menu at the bottom of the timeline. Use the other menus to adjust the date ranges shown in the bands: think of this as "zooming" in and out by choosing shorter or longer time periods. Enter text in the Filter box to display only references matching what you type. Type text into the four highlight boxes to mark matching references by color. The Fit to Screen button redraws the timeline to the current height of your browser window.

Notes

1. Center for History and New Media, "RTF scan..

2. Center for History and New Media, "Word processor plugin troubleshooting [Zotero Documentation]." Zotero, 2010. http://www.zotero.org/support/word_processor_plugin_troubleshooting.

3. For an introduction to editing Zotero styles, see http://www.zotero.org/support/csl_simple_edits.

4. "Styles."

5. Center for History and New Media, "Reports [Zotero Documentation]."

Further Reading

Center for History and New Media. "Reports [Zotero Documentation]." Zotero, 2009. http://www.zotero.org/support/reports.

———. "rtf_scan [Zotero Documentation]." Zotero, 2009. http://www.zotero.org/support/rtf_scan.

———. "Timelines [Zotero Documentation]." Zotero, 2009. http://www.zotero.org/support/timelines.

———. "Word processor plugin troubleshooting [Zotero Documentation]." Zotero, 2010. http://www.zotero.org/support/word_processor_plugin_troubleshooting.

"Styles." CitationStyles.org, 2010. http://citationstyles.org/styles.

CHAPTER 5 **Zotero Online**

So far, we've only used the Zotero "client"—the program installed on a single computer. As you've seen, the client software on its own is extremely useful, but in this chapter we'll look at ways to connect your Zotero library to the web, which adds an entirely new layer of features.

CHNM hit a significant milestone when they released Zotero version 2.0 in May 2009. This version represented a dramatic upgrade with two significant new features: synchronization and shared libraries. By creating an account on the Zotero website and connecting it with the local client software, references saved on the researcher's computer can be backed up and shared in new ways.

Synchronization (or "syncing") allows the researcher to automatically upload a copy of her library to the Zotero server online, kept current as references are added or deleted. This not only serves as a remote backup, but allows all of a user's computers to be tied to the same Zotero account so that the library is accessible from the home computer, office computer, and/or laptops.

Group libraries allow Zotero users to share work with each other: they are shared workspaces, public or private, separate from the single personal library. Group libraries can be coordinated by one person and shared with many, created and edited by many researchers simultaneously, or used as a private mutual workspace.

Any library, personal or group, that is synchronized with the Zotero servers can be easily published to the web as a means of sharing research.

Creating your Zotero Account

To get started, create an account on the Zotero website. This account serves a few functions. On the Zotero website, it allows you to create a profile including a photo and CV, view and share your library online, connect with other Zotero users, participate in the forums, and create and join group libraries.

Quick Steps: Set up Zotero Online

1. Go to zotero.org/user/register and register.
2. Open Zotero preferences, click the Sync tab.
3. Enter your username and password. Check Sync Automatically, click OK.
4. Click Sync button (circular green arrow).

In the Zotero client software on your computer, logging in with your account allows you to synchronize your library with the Zotero server and among all of your computers, save references to and from group libraries, and upload files to the Zotero Commons to share with researchers worldwide.

Go to Zotero .org and click "Register" (zotero.org/user/register). Follow the instructions: choose a username, enter your email and choose a password. Click the link in your email to confirm the new account.

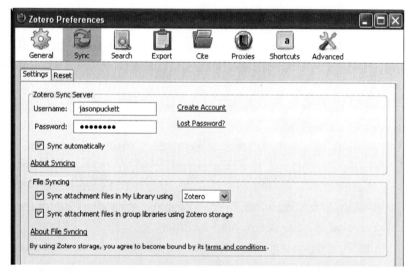

Figure 5.1: Enter your Zotero username and password on the Sync tab of the Preferences screen to synchronize your Zotero library across all your computers.

Once your account is set up, open Zotero, click the gear button and open the preferences screen. Click the Sync tab. Enter your username and password and make sure the Sync Automatically box is checked. Click OK.

Note that there are two places you'll enter your account information: on the website, and in the Zotero software itself. Logins do not carry over between the two: logging into the software does not log you into the website or vice versa.

Synchronizing your Library

Once you have your account set up and your username and password entered into the Zotero client, you can synchronize your library with the Zotero server. This feature allows you to take advantage of Zotero's free cloud storage to synchronize your library. (You can sync an unlimited number of references, notes and collections. PDFs and other attachments take up storage space, which is limited to 100MB for free. See "Attachment Storage" below.)

Synchronizing ("syncing") your library keeps it current by uploading any changes you make on your computer. If you use Zotero on multiple computers, it downloads any changes you have made from other computers as well.

Syncing has several advantages. As mentioned above, having access to the library from multiple computers is very handy. Even if you only work on a single computer, syncing also serves as an online backup of the entire library: the library is stored on your hard drive, but backed up on a remote server and easily restorable if the computer crashes.

Syncing in Action

Kate works on her desktop computer in her office on campus several times a week, but often does research and other work on her laptop from home or in the library.

Next time she's in the office, she enters her login information in Zotero on that computer and synchronizes it. She does the same to her laptop when she gets home.

They're now synchronized from now on: whatever changes she makes to her library on one computer automatically download to the other one the next time she opens Zotero.

Figure 5.2. Click the Sync button in the upper right corner to start synchronizing your library. The arrow spins while a sync is in progress; this happens automatically as you use Zotero. Mouse over the button to check the status of your sync.

If you disconnect from the internet, you still have a full copy of your library on your local computer. When you reconnect and open Zotero again, any changes you made while offline will synchronize.

Setting up synchronization also allows access to group libraries, about which much more shortly. Finally, any library set up for synchronization is easy to share online as desired. See "Publishing your library" later in this chapter for some ways to do this.

Enter your account info on the Sync tab of the Preferences screen as described above. In the upper right corner of the Zotero pane, click the circular green arrow button to start the synchronize process. This involves uploading your library to the Zotero servers, and downloading any references that you have previously synchronized from another computer. You'll only have to enter your login information once; Zotero "remembers" it from then on.

Note: Zotero and/or Firefox may freeze for a minute or two the first time you synchronize, especially if you have a large library with many attachments. This is normal: just get a cup of coffee and let it finish. Once you have syncing set up, it happens automatically in the background whenever you are connected to the internet and does not cause any noticeable lag. Zotero checks for any changes that need syncing the first time you open it, and synchronizes your library periodically as you make changes.

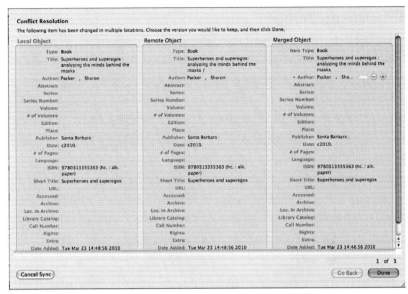

Figure 5.3. Resolve sync conflicts by choosing which version of the conflicted items you want to keep in your library.

The green arrow button will spin briefly from time to time as synchronization takes place (figure 5.2). Mouse over the button any time to see the sync status: whether a sync is currently taking place, and the last time the library was synchronized. If an error occurs during a sync, a red exclamation point appears to the left of the sync button. Click the exclamation point to see details of the error.

Resolving Sync Conflicts

Occasionally when syncing Zotero notifies you that one of your references has been changed on multiple computers.

If you edit a reference on two different computers before Zotero syncs them, a dialog will appear (figure 5.3) presenting the two versions of the reference and asking you to choose which version is the correct one, the local version (on your hard drive) or the remote one (on the server). Zotero also offers a "merged" choice that combines the changes made on both computers. Just choose the correct version by clicking it, and click Done.

Attachment Storage

Synchronizing backs up your attachments (such as PDFs) as well as citations. All Zotero users get 100 megabytes of free storage for attachment synchronization. This limit only applies to files attached to references: there is no limit on how many references can be synced. In other words, you can sync an unlimited number of citations, notes, and tags for free. You can sync up to 100 megs of PDFs, images, and web snapshots, and any other files attached to your references, for free. (More sync space can be purchased quite inexpensively at zotero.org/support/storage.)

Group libraries (see below) also sync attachments in some cases. Storage space for group files comes from the account of the group's owner, so if you own many active groups you may need to purchase more storage space.

Attachment syncing is enabled by default. Disable it from the Preferences/Sync tab if you prefer not to sync your attachments, either because of insufficient space or a slow network connection. Group file syncing can be disabled independently of your personal library.

Syncing attachments makes them accessible via your profile on the Zotero website. Log into the Zotero site, view your library at zotero.org/*yourname*/items, and click on any item with an attachment. At the bottom of a page you'll see a link to download the attached file. You must be logged into the Zotero site in order to download your attachments, or attachments in groups of which you are a member.

Your Library on the Web

Any library synchronized with the Zotero server is accessible from zotero.org. By default, your library remains private: no one can see it on the web except you. You can share your library publicly if you choose to: log into zotero.org, click Settings and then Privacy, and check the "Publish entire library" box. (You can also choose to publish your notes along with your library. Leave this second box unchecked if you want your notes to remain private.) Click Update.

Your library is visible from the My Library tab at the top left of the Zotero website (or zotero.org/*username*/items). Again, it is visible only to you unless you choose to publish it. From this page you can view your library from any browser, and on any computer without having to install Zotero.

The library is listed with the most recent additions first. Unlike in the Zotero client, no search feature is available. All of your collections are available as links to browse on the left side. Every collection also has a unique URL, so a librarian or instructor can easily create a list of references to share by saving them to a collection and sending a link.

Every item in the library has its own page; view details about any item by clicking its title. Attachments appear as links at the bottom of each reference under the heading "Notes and Attachments." Attached notes display the first line of text, and clicking this link shows the entire contents of the note. Some attachment types, such as snapshots, are not visible, although details about snapshots (URL and dates) do show up on the site.

You can download PDF attachments from your library. You must be logged in to access your attached PDFs even if your library is public. References with attached PDFs show two at the bottom of the page un-

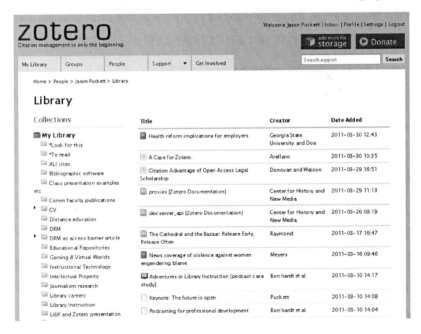

Figure 5.4. My personal library viewed on the Zotero website (zotero.org/username/items).

der Notes and Attachments: the filename (this link just displays details about the attachment) and a link that reads "pdf" followed by the size of the file. This second link goes to the actual PDF itself.

A library on the Zotero website is read-only: it's viewable, but not editable. Making changes to a library—adding citations, editing or deleting items, creating collections—requires accessing it from the client software. (This will change in future versions of Zotero, which will allow making edits via the website without needing to install the Zotero software.)

Group Libraries

Up to this point, you've saved all references into a single Zotero library: your personal library. Once you have connected Zotero to the internet, it becomes possible to create additional libraries shared with other researchers.

Each Zotero group has a shared library that may or may not be visible to non-members. Every group also has an information page on the Zotero website. Groups may be public or private. Private groups' information is only visible to group members who are logged into their Zotero accounts. Membership in public groups may also be either open, allowing anyone to join, or closed, requiring an invitation.[1]

Figure 5.5. The New Group button is next to the New Collection button at the top left of the Zotero window.

Creating a Group Library

To create a group, either browse to zotero.org/groups and click the "Create a new group" button, or open the Zotero pane and click the

New Group button, at the top left next to the New Collection button. Both open the "Create a new group" page on the Zotero site (you will be prompted to log in if you haven't logged into the site).

Choose a name for your new group. Public groups will be automatically be assigned a URL of zotero.org/groups/*groupname*. The "group URL" text below the name you enter will turn red if the name is unavailable or green if it is available. (Private groups can have any name.)

Next, choose the type of group: public (open or closed) or private. "Public" and "private" refer to the group's visibility by non-members, and "open" and "closed" indicate whether anyone can join the group or whether new members must be invited. A group can be changed between public and private, and public groups can be changed between open and closed, any time. (Private groups are always closed.)

What about Copyright?

Don't group libraries potentially provide a means to copy and share copyrighted files?

Yes. So does email. So does Facebook. So does the USB drive in your pocket. So does the postal service, for that matter.

Zotero makes no attempt to control what you choose to share in group libraries, any more than your email software polices your attachments for copyright violations. It's a neutral tool. You are still responsible for your own use of copyrighted information.

Public groups with open membership appear in Google search results and searches on the Zotero site. Any Zotero user can join a public group with open membership. Administrators can choose whether non-members can view the group library or specific collections. This kind of group is useful for sharing research in the broadest possible way: allowing anyone to join, view and copy references from the library. Group administrators can choose to allow members to add, edit and delete library items, or make the library read-only. Public open groups are the only type that cannot use group file storage.

Example: Nathan is a co-author on a shared blog about academic librarianship. He sets up a public Zotero group for blog authors and readers. Anyone can join the group, add and edit citations, and create collections. The blog's community uses it to share citations to works mentioned in posts and comment threads. The blog site includes a link to the group library's page so that anyone, not just group members, can view and save references from the library.

Public groups with closed membership appear in search results. Group members must be invited or approved for membership by the group's administrators. Administrators can choose whether non-members can view the group library or specific collections. This type of group is useful for work in which collaborators wish to show their research online, but control membership of the group.

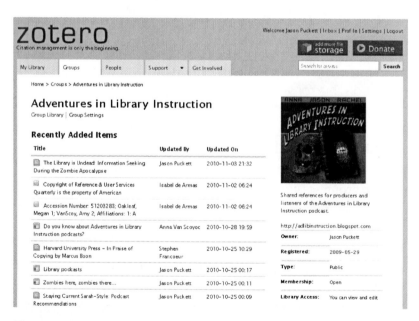

Figure 5.6. Web page for a public group library.

Example: Kate has assigned Ian's class a small-group bibliography assignment in which each member of the group must find four sources on their topic and produce a bibliography. Ian creates a public (closed membership) Zotero group and invites his two partners to join. All three group members can add references and see each others' references, and have Zotero format the bibliography when it's done. Kate can check in on the group's progress without having to be invited as a member.

Private groups are only visible to members, do not appear in search results, and members must be invited to join. Administrators can control whether members can add, edit and delete library items. Private groups are useful for collaborators who do not want to share their work outside of the group.

Example: Kate is collaborating on an article with a colleague in another state, and Anita is assisting with her research. She sets up a private group to create a workspace only the three of them can use. Kate saves citations to the group and tags them "needs pdf." Anita then sets up a saved search for this tag in her own Zotero client so she can see the article citations for which Kate wants copies. Once she's done that, she adds the PDFs as attachments to the references in the shared library.

Note: private group libraries and public groups with closed membership can be set to allow (or disallow) storage of file attachments. If attachments are allowed, the group uses storage space from the account of the group's owner, not the individual members. In other words, any PDFs saved to a group library by any member use up the group owner's free 100 megs of file space. Public groups with open membership cannot store attachment files, as a preventative measure to keep the owner's storage allowance from being used up.

Group Roles

Participants in a Zotero group occupy one of three roles: Owner, Admin or Member. A participant's role determines their level of control over the group's settings and content.

The creator of a group becomes its **owner**. The owner has full control over the settings of a group. If the group allows attachment storage, the space for attachment files comes from the owner's storage space on the Zotero server. The owner cannot leave a group without making someone else the owner first (see "Managing groups" below). The owner is the only one with the ability to change the type of group (private, public, open, closed) or delete it. (Any reference to group admins' abilities in this chapter refers to owners as well, since owners have all the same abilities as admins.)

Admins are group participants whom the owner has allowed to co-manage the group. They can change group settings, invite members, and control access to the library and file storage.

Members are the regular participants in a group. They can view the group's library, and depending on the group's settings, may be able to add, edit and delete library items and attachments.

MANAGING GROUPS

After creating a group you will land on its settings page. From this page, the owner and admins can set the options for the group. Only owners and admins see this page. The settings page has three tabs: Group, Members, and Library.

GROUP INFORMATION TAB

All information on the Group tab is optional except the name. Group information for public groups appears on the Zotero site and can be searched or browsed.

Name: This can be changed any time. Changing the name of a public group will change its URL as well.

Description: Enter a short description of the group's purpose or other descriptive information.

Disciplines: Select an academic subject area or areas relevant to the group.

Picture: Upload a picture that will appear on the group's public page.

Group URL: Enter the address of a website relevant to the group.

Comments: Checking this box allows comment posts to appear on the group's page in the form of a simple discussion board. See "The Zotero social network" later in this chapter for more about this feature.

This page also allows the owner to change the group type between public and private, or open and closed membership for public groups. The owner can delete the group using the button on this page.

After making any changes to the group information, click Save Settings at the bottom of the page.

MEMBERS TAB

This page allows the admins to invite, remove, and change the roles of group members.

Clicking the "Send more invitations" links near the top and bottom of this page allows admins to invite members. Enter email addresses or Zotero usernames into the top box. Any text entered into the bottom box will be included in the invitation email. Click Invite Members to send the invitations. Users can only join private groups by invitation.

The Current Members roster allows admins to change members' roles. Change a member to an admin or vice versa, or remove a member, by changing the drop-down menu in the right column. Save changes by clicking Update Roles at the bottom of the page.

The group owner can transfer ownership to any member (demoting herself to an admin) by choosing the username of the new owner from the dropdown menu and clicking Transfer. The new owner receives an email asking them to accept ownership (and transfer any group file storage to their own account). Until the new owner accepts, the previous owner can cancel the ownership transfer by clicking Cancel.

LIBRARY TAB

The Library page allows admins to control who can view and edit the library.

Library Reading: Select whether the library is visible to non-members via the Zotero website. This option appears for private groups as well, but has no effect: private libraries are never visible to non-members.

Library Editing: If this is set to "Only group admins," group members can view the library but not make changes to it. For most collaborative work, make sure to set this to "Any group member." Otherwise only admins will be able to save and edit references in the library.

File Editing: The "Any group member" setting allows all members to store attachment files in the library (again, this uses up the owner's storage allowance). The other options allow file storage access only to admins or disable it entirely. Public open groups cannot use file storage.

Joining Groups

Public groups appear in search results on the Zotero groups page. The search engine searches only the titles of groups, not the description, so if you want your groups to be easily discoverable choose their names carefully. (There is also a browsable list of all groups, but as it only offers an alphabetical list and there are nearly 12,000 public groups as I write this, it isn't very useful.)

A "Join Group" link appears on every public group's page (zotero.org/groups/*groupname*). Join the group by clicking the link. For open-membership groups, this immediately adds you to the group; for closed-membership groups, it notifies the group's owner of your request to join. The owner must approve your request before you can become a member. Users can only join private groups by an invitation from an admin.

On every Zotero user's profile page (zotero.org/*username*) there appears a menu labeled "Invite [user] to join one of your groups." This menu includes a list of all groups for which you are an admin. Invite the user to join a group by selecting the group name from the drop-down list and clicking Invite.

Group admins can also invite members from the "Send more invitations" link on the group's Settings/Members page. This is the best way to send multiple invitations at once, since the admin can paste in a list of email addresses or Zotero usernames.

Group invitations, and membership requests sent to group owners, appear in the Zotero inbox (zotero.org/message/inbox). This is usually forwarded to the user's email, but this behavior can be changed from the Email tab on the Settings page (zotero.org/settings/notifications). Invitations also appear on the Zotero groups page (zotero.org/groups) if you are logged into your account.

After you join a group, sync your library (click the green circular arrow button) to download the group's library. As always, syncing a large library may take a few minutes, so be patient if the group has a large shared library.

Use Case: Georgia State University Library

My institution is experimenting with a shared general-purpose group library (zotero.org/groups/georgia_state_university_library) for collaborative projects and reference sharing.

Our most recent application is a collaborative effort between subject librarians and the library's creative manager to create bibliographies and an online exhibit of books published last year by GSU faculty authors. Some librarians and staff are joining the group to act as editors and directly contribute material; those who don't use Zotero can send citations to a point person who enters the references. The project has offered learning opportunities for librarians and staff and made a few Zotero converts.

Future plans include creating collections of featured works by subject and piping them into LibGuides or elsewhere onto our website using the Zotero API.

The group is set to open/public; we consider the risk of "vandalism" (such as deleting important items) low, and we'll be encouraging GSU Zotero users from outside of the library to join and find their own uses for the group. One disadvantage is that the open/public setting doesn't allow attachments, so we will need to set up private or closed groups for other projects that require attaching files.

Using Group Libraries

You can interact with group libraries either via the Zotero software (the "client," the program you downloaded and installed) on your computer, or on the Zotero.org website. Each of the two interfaces allows different functions: in general, save and cite from the Zotero client software, and share information and control memberships and permissions using the website.

GROUP LIBRARIES IN THE ZOTERO CLIENT

If you are already comfortable using your personal Zotero library, using group libraries within the Zotero software will be very easy and familiar. If you are a member of a group and have syncing enabled, your group li-

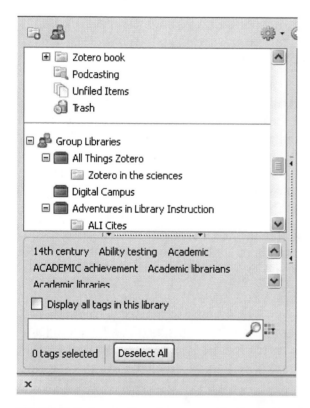

Figure 5.7. Group libraries appear in the left column, below your personal library and collections. Each box icon represents a library, which may or may not contain collections.

braries appear in the left column below your personal library. You should see My Library at the top of the column containing your collections, then a horizontal dividing line, then a Group Libraries heading and list of your group libraries with any collections they contain. (Below the group libraries appears another dividing line and a Commons heading. See "Zotero Commons" below.) You can always get back to your personal library by clicking "My Library" at the top of the left column.

Each group provides a library, separate from your personal library and from each other, containing its own set of references and collections. Think of each library as like a separate hard drive: they all appear in the same window on your computer, but they each contain their own files. You can copy and move items freely among them in most cases.

Whatever library or collection you select in the left column becomes the destination for new saved items. To save a citation to a group library, select the library or collection by clicking on it and then saving it from the catalog, database or website just as you would to save it to your personal library.

Working with these references is almost exactly like working with those in your personal library. To copy an item from My Library to a group library or vice versa, just select it in the center column and drag it to the library or collection in the left column. This creates a new copy of the item—changes made to an item in one library will not affect its copy in the other. Public groups with open membership cannot save attachments, so copying a reference with attached files into such a group will not copy its attachments. It will copy any attached notes, since notes do not use up file storage space.

Remember that some groups may allow members to view and copy references but may allow only admins to save and edit the library's contents (see "Managing groups" above). If you are unable to save or drag items into a group library (a "no" circle appears), check the group's permissions by viewing the group's web page.

GROUP LIBRARIES ON THE WEB

Every group has its own web page located at zotero.org/groups/*group-name* (although *groupname* will be replaced by a number for private libraries). Groups' web pages can serve as a public display for a collection of research material, a discussion forum, and a way to discover common research interests and share useful resources. Researchers can view group libraries on the web from any browser, and without installing the Zotero client software.

The group page displays the most recently added items to its library, a link to the entire group library, a link to its website, its owner and members. If you view a group's page while logged into zotero.org, your permissions for the group's library show next to "Library Access" in the right column: either "You can only view" or "You can view and edit." Members can see their private groups only when logged in.

Clicking the Groups tab on the Zotero site shows a list of all groups of which you are a member. Group libraries appear on the web at zotero.org/groups/*groupname*/items. A group library on the web includes all the features described in "Your library on the web" above. Logged-in group members can download attachments from the library's website.

Group libraries on the Zotero site have one extra feature: they include citation data to allow others to download the references. View a group library on the web, in a browser with Zotero installed. The Zotero capture icon—the yellow folder button—appears in the address bar, allowing anyone who can view the page to save citations from the library.

The Zotero Social Network

Creating a Zotero account gives you access to a simple social network. Zotero users can set up a profile page with information about themselves, link a Zotero collection as an online CV, send messages and hold group discussions, participate in the Zotero forums—or, of course, opt not to use any of these features.

Your Profile

Every user with an account at zotero.org has a public profile page at zotero.org/*username*. This profile contains no personal information, other than a list of any public groups of which the user is a member. You can use your profile as a place to publish information about yourself, your research interests, links to your website, and more.

Set up your profile by logging into the site and clicking Settings at the top right. The Profile tab on this page provides a space to enter your name, location, institutional affiliation, an "About You" paragraph, and a URL. The Disciplines list allows you to select one or more subject areas or professions in which you are interested (control- or command-click to select multiple areas). Upload a picture by clicking the Browse button at the bottom of the page, and save when done.

Your profile is searchable by Google and on the Zotero website (click the "People" tab and use the search box at the top right). Entering your institution, for example, allows anyone to search for the name of your university and find you. The People tab displays other users that share your subject interests if you chose a discipline in your profile. Including your real name provides an easy way for someone to locate you to invite you to join a group.

None of this information is required. If you prefer not to have search engines like Google discover your profile page, click the Privacy tab, check the "Hide from search engines" box and update your settings (or, of course, just don't enter any information into your profile).

Your CV

Click the CV tab (zotero.org/settings/cv). On this page it's possible to set up collections in your library as an online curriculum vitae that appears as a link on your profile (at zotero.org/*username*/cv). You build your online CV by saving citations to your own work in one or more collections in your personal library and then adding them via the interface on the Zotero site. Even if your library is private, you can choose to share only certain parts of it in your CV.

If you plan to use the Zotero CV feature, you should create one or more collections in which you save citations for your own work. You can create separate collections for books, articles, and presentations, or organize your work by subject—however you wish.

There are two types of elements available to add: *sections* that consist of a heading with text, or *collections* (a heading followed by the contents of one of your library collections). When you click the CV tab under your account settings, you should see a blank section. Click the

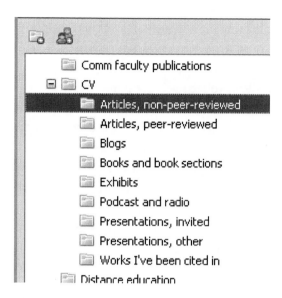

Figure 5.8. Collections to include in my online CV, viewed in the Zotero client.

heading, where you see light gray text reading "Enter a section name," and type the title of this section (such as "Employment history"). In the text box below, type whatever information you want: a list of your job history, for example. You can add links by selecting text and clicking the chain link icon.

Next, add a collection: Click "Insert a New Collection from Library." In the heading box that appears, type a title just as you did for the first section. Choose a collection from the drop-down menu below the heading. Click Save CV.

The green box that appears at the top of the page includes a link to your Zotero CV as it appears on your profile. There are no options for formatting: the CV appears in a generic style. (Future enhancements to this feature will include a choice of style.) If you need the CV in a particular bibliographic style, use Zotero to generate a bibliography and paste it into a text section.

Use the Move Up and Move Down buttons to reorder parts of the CV, and the Remove Section button to delete a section from the CV. Removing a section does not delete it from your library—it just takes it off your CV page.

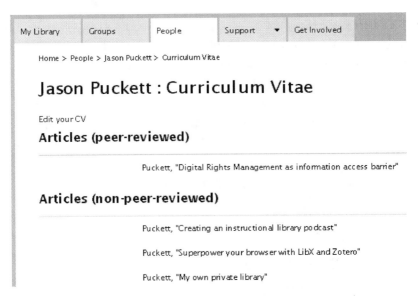

Figure 5.9: My CV viewed on the Zotero site (zotero.org/ username/cv)

Zotero Messages

Zotero accounts include the ability to send messages to other Zotero users, and to receive email notifications from the site.

Make sure your email address is correct under the Account tab. You can have multiple email addresses on file. Notifications will always go to the address marked Primary, which you can change at any time.

Click the Email tab to choose what events will notify you with an email: private messages from other users, new posts in group discussions, group invitations, applications to groups you own, or new followers to your account. It's probably a good idea to at least enable private messages and group applications so that you don't miss anything important, but you do can opt out of email notification entirely if you prefer.

Your Zotero inbox is located at zotero.org/message/inbox and is linked from the top of the Zotero site. From here you can see any notification messages you've received. Click Compose to send a message to any Zotero user, even if you don't have their email address. Any users whom you follow (see below) appear in your contact list on the right; select them from the list to compose a message to them.

Followers

As you browse other users' profiles, you may notice the "Follow" link on the right side of the profile page. Clicking this link adds this person to your "following" list and adds you to their "followers" list, both of which appear at the bottom of the profile page.

What does following someone do? Not a lot, honestly. It mostly provides a quick list of bookmarks to selected users on your profile page. This can be convenient because it:

- Gives you a list of links to Zotero users in whom you are somehow interested
- Provides an easy way to look at others' public libraries or invite them to groups
- Adds them to your Zotero contact list, which appears when you compose messages on the Zotero site

Browsing other users' follower lists can be a serendipitous way to discover others who share your research interests.

Discussion Features

The Zotero site includes two discussion features: the Zotero forums, and group discussions.

The Zotero forums (forums.zotero.org/categories) are public discussion boards. Anyone can post to the forums, which are read by CHNM staff as well as very knowledgeable users. These forums are an excellent place to get informed advice on any Zotero problems, suggest features, request new bibliographic citation styles, and so on. When posting a problem to the forums, make sure you provide as much information as possible and be prepared to answer specific questions about your setup, such as your operating system, browser version and so on. The forums are a vital resource for librarians and IT staff supporting Zotero as well as regular users.

Group discussions appear as a "mini-forum" at the bottom of each group page. Only members of the group can post, and topics are limited only by the members' wishes. Admins can turn the discussion feature on or off by checking the "Enable Comments" box on the group's settings page.

Zotero Commons

The Zotero Commons provides a free online repository for scholars to upload digital primary sources, images, or scholarly documents they have created. A partnership with the Internet Archive (archive.org) gives Zotero users a simple way to archive and share documents and images in the public domain or to which they own the copyright.

Quick Reference: Set Up Zotero Commons

1. Log into Zotero and click Settings/Commons.
2. Open archive.org in another window, click "join us" and create an account.
3. Open archive.org/account/s3.php, copy your access key and secret key and paste into your Zotero Commons settings.
4. Click Enable Commons.

Uploading materials to the Zotero Commons offers researchers several benefits. It provides a repository in which to share and discover resources, whether scanned public domain primary sources like historical newspapers or images, or secondary sources created by the researcher like bibliographies or finding aids. The Commons provides a stable long-term URL for other researchers to cite shared documents.[2]

The Internet Archive automatically processes any scanned files with Optical Character Recognition (OCR) software, placing a version of the document with searchable text in the user's Zotero library. Scholars who scan their own texts often do not have access to OCR software. The Internet Archive also automatically converts the file to several other standard formats: Zotero's native format, EPUB, Kindle, and others.

Since Commons items are stored on the Internet Archive, you'll need to create an account on the IA server. Open archive.org, click Join Us (at the top right of the page, next to the Upload button) and follow the instructions.

To connect your IA account to your Zotero account, go to Zotero Settings and click the Commons tab (zotero.org/settings/commons). You need to obtain your "S3 keys" from your IA account and paste them into the Commons settings page. These keys are like a username and password that allow your Zotero account to communicate with your IA account.

Open the URL archive.org/account/s3.php (the Commons Settings page has a link). Copy and paste the Access Key and Secret Key from the archive.org page into your Zotero Commons settings. Click Enable Commons.

Figure 5.10. The Internet Archive page for an item uploaded to Zotero Commons.

A globe icon labeled "Commons" appears below your group libraries in the Zotero software the next time it syncs. Create a collection to contain your uploads by right-clicking the Commons icon and choosing New Collection. Commons collections can take some time to create, so be patient.

Like group libraries, Commons collections are entirely separate from your personal library. Items can be dragged (copied) from group or personal libraries to Commons collections or vice versa. Drag an item from your personal library to your Commons collection to upload it.

Unlike group libraries, adding items to Commons collections takes some time—from ten minutes to several hours for the Internet Archive server to process the contribution before it appears in your Zotero client. During this time, the IA automatically checks to see if the item contains an image-only scanned PDF. If so, the PDF file will be run through its OCR software and converted to searchable text. A second copy of the PDF with "(OCR)" appended to the filename will be attached to the citation. This version of the PDF contains text that can be searched using the standard Zotero search features.

Items uploaded to the Commons also appear on the Internet Archive website—search by title or author within the Commons space on IA (archive.org/details/zoterocommons) to find them. Another benefit of uploading PDFs to the Commons is that the IA page for each item contains several different versions of each document: IA converts PDF documents to EPUB and other standard formats. The IA page also shows the number of times an item has been downloaded.

Publishing your Library

One of the main reasons to sync your library online is to publish it and share it with others—whether other Zotero users, your students or classmates, or other researchers working in your subject area. There are several ways to publish a Zotero library or collection, ranging from simply linking to a shared collection to more sophisticated options for publishing Zotero content to external websites.

Sharing Links

The simplest way to share a library online is simply to copy its URL. Every public Zotero library and collection, group and individual, has its own unique URL. Just browse to the library or collection on the Zotero website, copy the link from your browser address bar and share the link.

Libraries on the Zotero site include all the data that the Zotero client needs to save citations, so a researcher viewing a library on the web can save the citations to her own library. This can be handy for sharing citations for suggested reading with groups or classes.

Copy and Paste and HTML Bibliographies

The copy-and-paste method described in chapter 4 is a useful way to produce bibliographies to go into web pages. (Right-click library items or a collection, Create Bibliography, then select the desired style and choose "Copy to Clipboard." Paste into your web editor.) Bibliographies created in this way include COinS metadata —citation information visible to Zotero—that, like libraries viewed on the Zotero website, allows a Zotero user to save any of the citations from the web page.

Zotero can also produce bibliographies in HTML as described in the previous chapter. (Instead of clicking "Copy to Clipboard," choose "Save as HTML.") This creates a small, simple HTML file that can be pasted into any HTML editor. The HTML version lacks the COinS data that allows other Zotero users to save citations from the bibliography, however.

These two methods are good options for creating bibliographies for research guides like LibGuides or course management systems like Blackboard.

New Orleans Research Collaborative

The New Orleans Research Collaborative (nolaresearch.org) is a fantastic example of online collaboration using Zotero. The project centers around a number of New Orleans-related topics.

Undergraduates, grad students, librarians and faculty from Emory University, the University of New Orleans and other institutions contribute research and create bibliographies via Zotero group libraries. Students have the opportunity to participate in collaborative work early in their scholarly careers.

The bibliographies are vetted by an editor and updates are posted to the website periodically. Future plans include Omeka integration that will automate the publication process more fully.[3]

API and RSS: Feeding from Zotero to the Web

An Application Programming Interface (API) is a means for two computer programs to communicate with each other. For example, Google Maps has an API that allows other web applications to take its map data and add other information to it. Many popular applications that you've used, like YouTube, Flickr, and Twitter, have open APIs that allow them to feed content to other programs.

This feature will be greatly expanded in upcoming versions of Zotero, but without getting too technical let's look at a couple of simple examples of what it's capable of.

RSS

Every Zotero library and collection online generates an RSS (Really Simple Syndication) feed that can be used to push library updates to an RSS reader, blog or other RSS client. By default, items in the feed are not formatted in any bibliographic style—they just appear as a list of author name, title, and publication details as they appear in the right column of your Zotero library.[4]

Each online Zotero library or collection includes an orange RSS feed link labeled "Subscribe to this feed." Feed URLs must include a user or group number (an identifier associated with a Zotero account) and if the library is private, a key to access it. You can subscribe to the feed via an application like Google Reader, or push it into a compatible web application like LibGuides. (This section includes a few examples of how feeds can be customized. More detail is available on the Zotero site at zotero.org/support/dev/server_api.)

Feed URLs take the following forms:

- user library: **https://api.zotero.org/users/{userID}/items**
- user collection: **https://api.zotero.org/users/{userID}/items/ collections/{collectionKey}/items**
- group library: **https://api.zotero.org/groups/{groupID}/items**
- group collection: **https://api.zotero.org/groups/{groupID}/ collections/{collectionKey}/items**[5]

"userID" and "groupID" are numbers: find your userID at zotero. org/settings/keys. Group admins can get a group's ID by going to the group's Settings page: the groupID is the number after "groups/" in the URL (as in zotero.org/groups/**1234**/settings). To obtain a collectionKey, view the collection on the web and use the number after "collection/" in the URL (as in zotero.org/groups/groupname/items/collection/ **A1B2C3D4**). Your personal userID is visible at zotero.org/settings/keys.

Private libraries or collections require an API key (see below) for anyone else to access their feeds.

Note: Zotero generates secure (https) feeds. A few web applications—notably LibGuides, a program used by many libraries to create online research guides—are incompatible with secure RSS feeds. You can put a Zotero secure feed URL into a program like Yahoo! Pipes (pipes.yahoo.com) or Feedburner (feedburner.google.com) to convert it from secure to non-secure RSS.

API Keys

RSS feeds are one use of the API. Other applications can use data generated by the API: for example, the Bibliobouts game mentioned in chapter 6 uses API data to read the contents of a group library. Private libraries and collections require a key—a code provided by the library's owner—to share their contents. Zotero uses a protocol called OAuth to provide secure communication.

A private key is a code that allows Zotero to share the contents of even a private library, if the owner wishes. You can create keys that permit access to an entire library or just part of it. Go to your Settings page and click the Feeds/API tab (zotero.org/settings/keys). Click "Create new private key."

On this page you can enter a description for the key (choose any name you want, like "Key to my personal library") and select what data you want the API to be able to access: your personal library, your notes, all your groups or individual groups you own. Click "Save Key." You can edit an existing key on this page to change its access permissions.

Your Feeds/API tab now shows a list of any keys you have created. The key itself is a long string of letters and numbers that can serve as a password to access a private RSS feed (see above). It looks something like: **x1yzml1ca5spmew136xo4yy6**.

To add a key to an RSS feed or other API URL, just add **?key=** plus the key itself to the end of the URL, like: **https://api.zotero.org/users/475425/collections/9KH9TNSJ/items?key= x1yzml1ca5spmew136xo4yy6**

API Example: Generating a Bibliography in Libguides

LibGuides is a popular web application for librarians to create online research guides. One use for the Zotero API is creating collections to automatically appear as bibliographies in a LibGuides box.

Start to create a bibliography from a collection by assembling a URL as noted in the RSS section above. For example: **https://api.zotero.org/ users/475425/collections/9KH9TNSJ/items** gives an RSS feed for the contents of Zotero user number 475425's collection number 9KH9TNSJ. (Of course, you'll substitute your user number from zotero.org/settings/ keys and the number from your collection's URL.)

You can instruct Zotero to give you the information in a format other than RSS, though. Add a question mark (?) to the end of the URL, followed by some additional options. For example, to change that RSS feed to a formatted bibliography, add **?format=bib**:

https://api.zotero.org/users/475425/collections/9KH9TNSJ/ items?format=bib

Typing that URL into a browser window returns a short bibliography in Chicago style. You can add additional options: add an ampersand (&) to the end of the URL between each parameter and string more options onto the end of the URL. For example, to change styles from Chicago to APA, add **&style=apa**:

https://api.zotero.org/users/475425/collections/9KH9TNSJ/ items?format=bib&style=apa

You can format the output in any of the default Zotero styles by changing the "apa" to the filename of the desired style (like "mla" or "nature" for example). If the library is private, you will need to add an API key with **&key=*[key number]*** at the end.

To add this bibliography to a LibGuide, create a Remote Script box in your guide. Copy the API URL you have created, click "Add/Edit the Remote Script URL" and paste it into the box. The guide will show the contents of the collection as a bibliography formatted in APA. As you add and edit items in the collection, periodically the bibliography on your guide will refresh itself to show your updates.

This is just one *very* simple example of what's possible with the Zotero API, and I've only shown a couple of the many options available. CHNM will be focusing on the API and adding many new and exciting possibilities to this feature in the near future, so expect new features to be available. Plugins either are, or will soon be, available to use Zotero data in Wordpress, Omeka and other content management systems. I've also only covered the "read API"—the system that allows Zotero to push information into other applications. The new "write API" will allow third-party applications to create and modify Zotero items, collections, and notes. Web librarians and developers should take a look at zotero.org/support/dev/server_api for the latest information.

Notes

1. The bibliographies for all chapters of this book are available in a public group library at zotero.org/groups/z_guide_by_puckett.
2. Cohen, Dan. "Zotero and the Internet Archive Join Forces." *Dan Cohen's Digital Humanities Blog*, December 12, 2007. http://www.dancohen.org/2007/12/12/zotero-and-the-internet-archive-join-forces/.
3. New Orleans Research Collaborative. "About." *New Orleans Research Collaborative*, 2010. http://nolaresearch.org/about.
4. I'm using the more familiar term "RSS," but technically speaking, Zotero delivers its data in ATOM and JSON formats that can be read by RSS-capable applications.
5. Center for History and New Media, "Plugins/ZoteroImport—Omeka How To." *Omeka*, 2010. http://omeka.org/codex/Plugins/ZoteroImport.

Further Reading

Center for History and New Media. "commons [Zotero Documentation]." Zotero, 2010. http://www.zotero.org/support/commons.

———. "dev:server_api [Zotero Documentation]." *Zotero*, 2011. http://www.zotero.org/support/dev/server_api.

Cohen, Laura. "Library 2.0: An Academic's Perspective: Zotero Commons: Who Needs Libraries?" *Library 2.0: An academic's perspective*, n.d. http://liblogs.albany.edu/library20/2007/12/zotero_commons_who_needs_libra.html.

Johnston, Lisa R. "Let's Get Social, Cite me?" *Sci-Tech News* 62, no. 4 (November 2008): 30.

CHAPTER 6 Teaching Zotero

Teaching Zotero can take place in many contexts: in an in-person workshop, as part of a library instruction session, as part of a graded course assignment, or in online classes. Zotero may be the main focus of a class session or only one element of a research exercise. Our library regularly teaches Zotero in hour-long workshops, in hands-on "research lab" sessions, and five-minute demo sessions.

Teaching a reference manager program is like teaching any other research tool, and planning a Zotero class is fundamentally no different from planning any other information literacy class. Consider the information needs of the audience, how their past experience is likely to inform their learning, plan some specific learning objectives, and know the material well enough to be flexible and respond to the unexpected.

This chapter presents suggested best practices from my own experience teaching Zotero, as well as advice and real-world assignments and examples from other Zotero instructors (both librarians and teaching faculty).

Classroom Preparation

Many library classes only require a working web browser, since so many research tools now exist as online tools like catalogs and article databases. Demonstrating Zotero requires a few pieces of software in working order: the browser (probably Firefox), the Zotero client software (Firefox add-on, standalone application or possibly both), and probably the Microsoft Word toolbar plugin.

Even if you plan to demonstrate installing Zotero "live" during class, pre-install and test the software on the actual computer you will use for teaching, and allow enough time to deal with unexpected problems before students arrive. A test drive on your own office computer may be a good practice run, but try it out on the classroom computer. Having Zotero pre-installed also allows you to give a demonstration at the very beginning of class.

Public use computers and classroom computers often have security settings that prevent users from installing new software. These security measures often still allow the user sufficient permissions to install the Firefox plugin version of Zotero and possibly the Word toolbar as well. Allowing students to install Zotero themselves during class as a hands-on exercise is useful if time permits, since it gives them experience with the procedure before they go home to try it on their own. It does take a few extra minutes of class time, however, and may be impractical depending on your classroom computers' security settings.

On many campuses, library and classroom computers are protected by Deep Freeze or similar software that "undoes" any changes made to the system when it reboots. Of course this wipes out any Zotero installation, saved data and updated versions between classes, so remember to coordinate appropriately with your IT department. If your classroom does not use software like this, test your Zotero setup to make sure another instructor has not made any changes since your last workshop. I usually give our instructor computers a "Zotero checkup" a week or so before my first class of the semester to make sure all is in working order; this gives me time to request that our IT department install any needed updates.

Make a separate Zotero account just for teaching, and keep that account's library small, with only a few references. This keeps your teaching examples out of your personal library and vice versa, and keeps sync time short during class demonstrations. If you join any public groups with that account, make sure not to save any irrelevant items to the group libraries during class activities.

I usually encourage learners to bring their own laptops to workshops if they wish. You may not have any other option if you lack a classroom space with dedicated computers, or are teaching in an unusual setting like a conference session. "Bring your own laptop" has the advantage of allowing the student to work on a computer without security restrictions and with which they are already comfortable, and also allows them to install Zotero on their own computer with experienced help available. This may cause trouble for the instructor, in the form of troubleshooting problems on unfamiliar computers and operating systems, outdated or incompatible software, while the rest of the class waits. For example, my Zotero workshop announcements have always specified that Firefox is required on any laptops they bring to class, but students still turn up without it installed.

Consider the Audience

Begin planning a Zotero class by giving some thought to the expected audience. The research experience and information needs of a first-year undergraduate class are entirely different from those of a group of PhD students, and each group will pick up the concepts and skills differently.

Consider what features will be the most important to each group— what they most need to know (and already know) how to do for their current research assignments. If the class has a professor or group leader (not the case in a drop-in workshop), ask him for a little information about this semester's assignment and how far along they are likely to be. Don't forget to also consider what you know about the class's likely comfort level with technology in general: facility with word processor and browser features (notably installing add-ins), and simple computer literacy skills like switching between windows and copy/paste will come into play.

Plan a few learning outcomes bearing all this information in mind. It may be impossible to teach everything they need and answer every question in a single session (librarians who have been asked to "give a general library overview" in a 50-minute class already know this painful truth). Give them enough information and experience to accomplish the basics of what they need, explain that experience will raise more questions and improve their comfort with the software, and make sure they know where to get help after class.

I'll present several common audiences for Zotero classes, starting with an unknown drop-in audience and then progressing in assumed increasing experience and sophistication with research tools: undergrads, grad students, faculty and librarians. The suggested material for lower-level groups can probably be covered in a shorter time, requiring less explanation, so it's usually practical to cover more features with more advanced researchers.[1] If your audience includes other groups, hopefully these examples will give you ideas of how to approach planning for them.

Be prepared to answer more advanced questions, but don't confuse new users with too much information. Keep a mental eye on what they need from the software based on what you know of your audience and their questions during class. You don't have to (and can't possibly) have answers to all the questions prepared in advance; just know more than your students and you'll be fine. A sense of FAQs and common problems will come with experience, just like teaching any other kind of class.

Also be prepared to say "I don't know" and follow up after rather than stall the class trying to fix a problem. If you can, it's often helpful to block off a few extra minutes on your calendar to help with individual problems and questions immediately after class.

The Basic Zotero Workshop

This outline is a good basic structure for teaching Zotero to almost any audience. Specific audiences will likely have particular questions and concerns, but for the most part adapting this model just requires making adjustments of how much time and which features to cover and omit based on your own knowledge of your learners' needs. Be flexible! (See Appendix A for sample handouts.)

Basic Workshop Outline
- Quick demo
- Installation
- Saving citations
- Creating bibliographies
- Synchronization

Begin the session with a brief explanation of what Zotero is and what it can do. Don't bother with a discussion of open source software unless you know that would interest your audience, but do at least mention that Zotero is free for anyone to download.

Start with a brief demonstration as described in "the 'Wow' moment" sidebar below. Don't try to explain *how* to do anything at this point—that's what the rest of the hour is for—but use this moment to show how useful Zotero can be. Open the library catalog or a database, ask someone in the audience for their current research topic and do a quick search (don't worry about getting the best quality results, just find some citations to save). Save some results, pointing out the notification _ popup as you do so. Open the Zotero library to show the saved items and use the Create Bibliography menu item to paste a quick bibliography into Word.

From here, move into step-by-step hands-on practice mode. Cover installation, saving and editing items, creating bibliographies via copy/paste and with the Word plugin, and possibly synchronization and group libraries. Take a moment during each process to check in for questions and problems: explicitly ask something like "Did that work for everyone? Did anyone have trouble?". Most of these activities build on the previous ones, and nothing is more frustrating for you or the rest of the class than finishing a practice activity of saving citations to find that someone got lost while installing Zotero but was too embarrassed to say so. Physically walking around the classroom to check in on students during activities is very helpful.

Decide ahead of time whether to pre-install Zotero on your classroom computers. If you decide to pre-install Zotero to save time, at least demonstrate the process briefly yourself; many people have never installed software or even a browser plugin by themselves. Provide a handout or guide with the URLs and instructions. If you have students

---

The "Wow" Moment

I start every Zotero class with a quick demonstration of saving citations and using the copy-paste method to create a bibliography. I don't explain **how** to do it yet, I just show **what** it can do.

When I click Paste in Word and the finished bibliography appears —only a few seconds after saving citations from the catalog—the audience always murmurs excitedly, and I usually hear some impressed interjections and some comments like "I wish I had known about this when I was a freshman!" (And, on at least one occasion, enthusiastic profanity.)

I think of this as the "Wow" moment in every class. It never fails to demonstrate to researchers, much more effectively than I could explain to them verbally, just how much time and work Zotero can save. It's the best way to get their attention at the beginning of class.

install Zotero themselves, check to make sure everyone has succeeded before you proceed.

Installing the word processor toolbar is often more confusing since it involves clicking through to the installation page and choosing the correct version. Mac users also have to deal with the extra step of installing the correct PythonExt version along with the plugin, so allow a few extra minutes to circulate and help. This is usually the longest "pause and check in" during the session. Again, physically walk through the classroom if possible, glance at everyone's screens and help with individual problems. Once the software is installed, open Zotero and briefly explain the three columns: left side for browsing collections and tags, middle for a list of citations and the right to display and edit details.

Saving citations is one of the most important features, but fortunately quite easy to teach and learn. Have students open the library catalog and ask them to try a search of their choice, then click on the first result. Point out the book icon in the address bar: explain that Zotero scans web pages as they loads and indicates citations by adding a save button appropriate to whatever items it detects. Point out the pop-up notification as you save a catalog citation.

This point in class is where librarians are invariably tempted to slip into library jargon without realizing it. Unless your audience is made up of librarians, avoid terms like "record" (as in catalog or database record), "metadata," and "fields." Use more common terms like "page" or "citation" (as in "this book's page/citation in the catalog"), and "tags" or even just "information" (as in "Zotero saves the information about this article," or "Zotero tags the item with author and title and publication details").

Open Zotero to point out the new saved citation, mentioning that Zotero continues to run in the background whether the browser pane is open or closed. (Check in: Did everyone successfully save a citation?) Now that you have a citation in the library, demonstrate the ease of editing the item by just clicking the text to edit.

Repeat the save exercise in an article database, pointing out the different capture icon for different reference types (books, articles, book chapters), and make sure to demonstrate saving multiple citations from a list of search results. Don't assume that everyone in the class knows how to get to the library's databases: be prepared to talk through the steps to get there slowly and assist lagging students. If the group is from the same academic department, choose a database from their discipline to demonstrate: the exercise will seem much more relevant to them if they are using familiar sources in conjunction with Zotero.

Almost invariably, questions arise at this point about attaching PDFs to citations. Show the preference setting to automatically attach PDFs when possible, but make sure students know that this only works for a small number of databases. Demonstrate the drag-and-drop method of attaching PDFs.

Save a citation from a web site. Take a look at the attached snapshot, explaining that this is just another kind of attachment. Make sure to point out what information Zotero does *not* save when capturing web citations: author and date are usually key.

Once students have some items in their library, demonstrate how to organize them into collections. Point out that items can be in more than one collection simultaneously. This is also a good time to demonstrate tagging and browsing by tag.

When teaching how to create bibliographies, consider the audience—some groups may be content with the copy/paste bibliography method, some may be more interested in the Word toolbar, or you may want to demonstrate both. Make sure that the group gets some hands-on experience with at least one of the two methods. Often, demonstrating the copy/paste method generates questions about whether Zotero can create in-text citations or footnotes as well. (For some reason, having Zotero create footnotes never fails to impress.)

If you have students create a Zotero account and set up synchronization in class, spend a few minutes demonstrating how to get to the Sync tab in the Zotero preferences, circulating around the classroom and helping them enter their account information.

As noted above under Classroom Preparation, create a Zotero account just for teaching, and keep that library empty or nearly so. This keeps the sync process relatively quick and keeps your teaching examples from cluttering your personal library. Syncing for the first time may hang the browser up briefly. Don't panic when that happens; start the sync process on your screen and use this time to circulate and check in as they set up their own accounts.

Depending on the audience, this may be a good time to cover group libraries. There's not much to demonstrate visually here: explain the concept, show how to set up a group on the website, and point out where group libraries appear below the personal library in the Zotero client. Drag and copy some references back and forth between group and personal libraries—but only if you have a suitable practice group set up. Don't clutter anyone's "real" public group library with your teaching examples, of course.

Close by briefly mentioning any other features you didn't have time for during the session—anything that your audience might think of as "advanced" but that would be interesting or useful to them. Make sure to give them a handout for later reference, a URL to your online guides, and your contact information for later support questions.

You can easily adapt this basic model for different audiences and teaching situations.

Drop-in Audiences

Many libraries offer drop-in Zotero workshops open to anyone from undergrads to faculty to members of the public. The trouble with planning workshops like this is that it's impossible to know ahead of time who your audience will be. Their familiarity with bibliographies, library research resources, and computers in general can make a big difference in how the class goes. An experienced researcher who has used EndNote or RefWorks for several years will pick up the fundamentals of Zotero much more quickly than a first-year student who has only a vague idea of the purpose of bibliographies. Instructors of drop-in workshops should be prepared to handle a spectrum of learners in the same class (and just to make it interesting, expect someone to bring a new laptop with an operating system they're still learning to use).

The goal for drop-in workshops should be to cover enough features and techniques in one hour that users can walk away and use Zotero usefully, even if they don't see every feature. Since it's hard to predict ahead of time who will attend, build some flexibility into the plan. Assume that at least some attendees will be novice researchers (perhaps even first-time library users if the session takes place at the beginning of fall semester), but be prepared to address more advanced features if learners ask questions about them.

Requiring or encouraging pre-registration may help give you an idea of who will be attending. In any case asking questions at the beginning of class is useful: your learners' status as faculty or students, what disciplines they are studying, favorite databases, and previous experience with Zotero or other reference managers. Our classroom contains all Windows computers, so I try to remember to ask if anyone in the session is a Mac user so that I can point out differences and mention the extra steps in installing the Word plugin.

The Five-minute Demo

Sometimes circumstances dictate teaching less than a full class session: either a Zotero "guest spot" in someone else's class or a short demonstration as a side note to a class on another topic. I often add five minutes' worth of impromptu Zotero information to the end of "regular" information literacy sessions. A few minutes can be plenty of time to engage learners' interest. If you only have a brief window of time in which to demonstrate Zotero, keep a few things in mind:

My five-minute demos usually consist of installing Zotero, going to the library catalog site, saving some citations, pasting a quick bibliography into word, answering questions and sharing the URL to my online guide. Don't forget to mention any upcoming workshops or online tutorial videos available.

Don't spend more than a sentence or two explaining what Zotero is and what it does before you start. Perhaps ask whether students have used reference manager software before just to get an idea of how much explanation might be helpful.

Don't try to teach any step-by-step processes. Engage their attention quickly. The best way to do that is to go straight for the "Wow" moment (see sidebar above): just save some citations and create a copy/paste bibliography. (Ideally, have your word processor already open in another window before you start. Nothing kills the pace of a quick demo quite like waiting for Word to load.) Showing this visual, practical demonstration always captures learners' interest. Expect questions to follow quickly.[3]

Sample Assignment: Second-year English

Oregon State University Librarian and English instructor Anne-Marie Dietering assigns a bibliography project using Zotero as part of a literary research course. She requires students to cite, annotate and tag three sources in their personal libraries and add them to a class group library for grading.

The assignment and Dietering's reflections on developing it are available on her blog.[2] She hopes that "showing them Zotero pushes their brains beyond the 'research skills is what you have to do to do well on this specific paper' focus that most one-shot sessions have. I try and frame it as a life skill for students ... that part of college is building this personal knowledge base."

Abandon any plans to include hands-on activities. Although this is the best way to get comfortable with Zotero, there just won't be time to more than whet their interest and answer questions. If everyone has laptops already online, the group is comfortable with their computers, and has Firefox already installed, you might just have time to walk students through the installation process so that they can take Zotero home with them.

If you do have more than a few minutes, consider what elements you might want to add from the drop-in workshop class model. The essentials to consider demonstrating include saving and editing items, creating bibliographies using copy/paste, and creating collections. At least mention the ability to synchronize and share libraries online.

Regular Library Instruction Sessions

If Zotero isn't the primary focus of a class, it can be incorporated as an additional learning outcome. This can be particularly effective with library instruction sessions for upper-division undergraduate classes.

Often these students have "had the library class before," and showing them a new tool can help get past their initial resistance to sitting through another library session.

Of course, make sure you know the class's assignment and the search tools they need to use. Make sure the databases you plan to teach work well with Zotero—or if they don't, be prepared to answer questions about potential problems. If students have their own computers, or you are a guest in their regular classroom instead of your usual teaching space, check on the available technology.

Use the five-minute demo model at the beginning of class. As you teach different search tools, demonstrate how to save citations and point out any idiosyncrasies or problems you might have discovered using Zotero with those particular databases. If students are not using their own laptops in class, make sure they have time to synchronize their library or export it to a flash drive before class ends.

Undergraduate Students

When teaching first- and second-year undergraduates, focus on the basic functions to get them comfortable with Zotero as a research tool. A typical undergraduate class may have a short research assignment with a bibliography. They probably need to cite some books, some articles, and possibly some web sources as well. Few of the students have delved very deep into library research yet, and some of them may not have done a bibliography for a college paper before.

Zotero Learner: Ian, Undergraduate

Ian's first-year class has a short research paper due based on book , article and web sources. Suggested learning outcomes for his class's Zotero session include:
- Installing Zotero
- Saving citations (catalog, database, web)
- Creating bibliographies by copy/paste

This is their first exposure to bibliography software. In planning this session, Nathan will probably omit the Word toolbar and syncing unless asked about them, and won't mention group libraries unless he knows that they have a group assignment this semester.

Their immediate needs for Zotero are saving citations and creating bibliographies. They are taking required classes in several disciplines, so the ability to create bibliographies in many different styles is useful.

Lower-division undergrad students are early in their academic careers. They may not see advantages in building a long-term personal library, since at this point they are unlikely to have discovered ongoing research interests, but they will quickly grasp the idea of Zotero as a labor-saving tool for creating bibliographies. Undergraduates have many conflicting demands on their time and energy and appreciate anything easy and efficient that can help ease their workload.

Upper-division undergraduates have chosen a major and have more research experience under their belts. Students at this level will be able to draw on their past work in thinking about potential uses, and will likely have more specific questions about which resources work with Zotero.[4] Expect questions about how Zotero works with particular databases from audiences starting with experienced undergrads all the way through faculty learners. These populations all have their favorite go-to information sources and will want to try them out with Zotero. Consider teaching additional features like using the Word toolbar and synchronizing libraries.

Sample Assignment: Third-year Political Science

Georgia State University Political Science professor Mike Evans has his students contribute to a shared Zotero library as they do research. Students learn Zotero from the subject librarian during a one-shot library instruction session and follow up with Evans during the semester for technical help.

"Zotero's great advantage was in allowing me to see their work and give them feedback before they turned in the assignment. ... I was able to observe most students building their bibliographies in 'real time.'" Evans says.

Students did not print out and turn in a formatted bibliography—they submitted the assignment by copying references to individual collections within the class library.

One advantage of teaching Zotero in particular to undergraduates is that its barriers to entry are low. You can demonstrate the basic functions they need, saving and citing, in just a few minutes. While more advanced features are available if needed, this is often overkill for undergraduates: one reference manager study by academic librarians found that the commercial software they tested had "an extensive learning curve, and perform unnecessary functions for undergraduate assignments."[5] Zotero's relatively easy learning curve serves as an easier introduction to bibliography software.

Don't give in to the stereotype of assuming that all young students are technologically proficient. Any group—of any age—to whom you present is likely to include a spectrum of confidence and knowledge with technology. Undergraduates may have grown up with ubiquitous technology in their lives, but some may not know which web browser they use or have experience installing software. Don't gloss over fundamental concepts too quickly.

Do stress the need to proofread the final product. Explain that no software will be able to create a one hundred percent accurate bibliography; during demonstrations, point out elements that need correction (Zotero almost always saves at least one citation with capitalization or punctuation that must be tweaked). My students always hear "Don't trust a computer to make your bibliography" at least once. Another useful phrase is "garbage in, garbage out": saving citations without checking them over results in incorrect bibliographies. Responsibility for correctly making the bibliography still rests with the students, and as instructors we share the responsibility for making that point clear.[6]

Sample Activities for Undergraduate Classes

Instructors of undergraduate courses may wish to incorporate Zotero activities into graded assignments. Some examples from actual librarians and faculty members appear in sidebars in this chapter, but some ideas to consider include:

- Sharing students' individual sources with peers or with the instructor as they do research. This could be done either with a class group library with collections created by students, or by having students share access to their personal libraries. (The professor can even check dates added and modified for each source if she wishes to discourage last-minute research.)

- Conducting small group collaborative research. This is an obvious application for the group library feature: each group creates a Zotero group library in order to pool resources. One student may be designated "research director" and put in charge of coordinating the Zotero library, or duties could be shared.
- Building shared libraries as part of a class-wide project. The instructor creates a group library and directs the class's research as students add sources and collections over the course of a semester. The finished product can be put online as a resource for future researchers. For a very ambitious long-term collaborative project along these lines, see "New Orleans Research Collaborative" on page 136.
- Any of these examples could incorporate an element of peer research evaluation. Any library shared online can be made available for the rest of the class to add comments, additional sources and suggestions if the instructor wishes to strengthen the collaborative aspect of the research project.

These ideas might work particularly well with distance education classes, in which opportunities for online student and group interaction are particularly valuable.

Grad Students

Graduate students are likely to appreciate Zotero's potential as a repository for their ongoing research as well as an organizational tool for multiple research projects. (See Appendix B for Zotero Online Features handout.) Many grad students have the long-term goal of a thesis looming over them and will certainly have a sustained research interest or two. Add to that the prospect of additional coursework with research papers, and Zotero is an easy sell. In many ways, a graduate student group is my favorite audience for Zotero. They have enough

BiblioBouts

BiblioBouts (bibliobouts.org) is a game developed by the University of Michigan. Students install Zotero, create BiblioBouts accounts, and allow the BiblioBouts application to read items from their personal libraries.

Players (typically undergrad students) select sources on their assigned topic by saving them in Zotero, evaluate their peers' selected sources for quality and relevance, and construct a bibliography based on the class's pooled sources.

Winning the game requires meeting criteria set by the instructor, agreeing with classmates' ratings of sources' quality, and contributing sources that make the cut as choices for final bibliographies.[7]

research experience to immediately grasp its value, enough knowledge to ask useful questions, and usually enough comfort with technology to figure out the basics quickly and move on to practical applications.

Gather any information you can about the research needs of the students before you meet, and plan to discuss their projects with them during class; possible applications for Zotero may suggest themselves during the conversation. For students in disciplines like history and literature, be aware of the primary sources they might be using, and how Zotero interacts with their databases of choice. Students using unique or archival sources may need to enter them by hand.

Zotero Learner: Anita, Grad Student

Anita's class is working on a long paper involving some primary source research. Nathan plans to teach them:

- Installation
- Saving and editing citations
- Creating collections
- Entering citations by hand
- Attaching PDFs
- Creating bibliographies by copy/paste and Word toolbar
- Synchronizing

He plans to demonstrate other advanced features as they come up in questions and discussion.

Sample Assignment: First-Year Library Science Graduate Students

Kathryn Greenhill, Associate Lecturer in Information and Library Studies at Curtin University of Technology, assigns a Zotero exercise to her Information Management Technologies course, a required first-year class aimed at building library science students' technology competencies.

Students create an annotated bibliography with a prescribed variety of references (websites, articles, books) using metadata saved from a given list of search tools (including Google, Google Scholar, Wikipedia, LISTA, and other scholarly databases).

They are required to manually clean up references' metadata, add DOIs and other missing information, attach PDF articles, format the bibliography in APA style in Word and annotate each entry. They document their use of Zotero by creating screenshots that accompany the final assignment.

This assignment includes not only a research component, but gives students practical experience using Zotero with a variety of reference types and online research tools.

Suggested learning outcomes for a grad student class include the basic saving and citing functions, but also creating collections, manipulating attachments, syncing and possibly group libraries. They will definitely have favorite databases and other online research tools and will likely ask specific questions about their interaction with Zotero. Their questions often take the form "Can Zotero do X?", so be prepared to discuss functions not on the original lesson plan.

Grad students appreciate Zotero's ability to save PDFs to their library and to synchronize attachments online for when they use other computers—or at least as a secure backup. (They often save sources during Zotero workshops that they wish to take with them.) Walk them through creating accounts and setting up synchronization. Plan to include a demonstration of attaching files, and note which databases in their field can auto-attach PDFs. Group libraries may be useful if their class is doing collaborative work.

Hands-on "lab"-style sessions often work well with students at this level since they have a real interest in their immediate information need: if time permits, spend the first part of class showing the basics and then allow them some free time to experiment. Address questions by demonstrating features on your projected screen so the whole group can see, as questions and discussion suggest. If this group is a course with a professor present for the session, ask for input and include her in the discussion. (The professor is often at least as interested in Zotero as the students are.)

Faculty and Librarians

I usually approach teaching these two groups similarly. Both academic librarians and teaching faculty typically have their own ongoing research interests, so (unlike undergraduates) the usefulness of a personally curated library of citations usually appeals. Both groups assist up and coming researchers to some degree, so may be interested in how to use Zotero in the classroom. They may have their own IT staff who can set up Zotero for them, or may be doing research on their home laptops. They are probably engaging in collaborative work to some degree, either with colleagues or students, so groups and syncing are useful.

A workshop for this group can follow roughly the same plan as that for grad students. Faculty of course have their own focused interest in a particular discipline, so if you have a group from the same department, plan to demonstrate Zotero using databases from their subject. Librar-

---

Zotero Learner: Kate, Teaching Faculty

Kate's department has invited Nathan to present a Zotero workshop as part of their brownbag learning series. Nathan expects to include some of the following in addition to the basic save and cite features:

- Saving citations from any discipline-specific databases this group might use
- Synchronization and group libraries
- Downloading major styles for journals in their field
- Scanning PDFs for metadata via Google Scholar
- Discussion of classroom uses

---

ians might be likely to represent a range of disciplines, since a group of subject librarians probably support researchers from many subjects. Ask if there are any particular databases or catalogs your group would like to see demonstrated when saving citations; seeing Zotero interact with their familiar research tools helps showcase its practicality in a relevant way.

Like grad students, librarians and faculty have favorite databases and research tools, and will probably veer off on their own during class to try out Zotero with Project Muse or JSTOR or PubMed, or their own library catalog or online archive, to see how well it can save citations. Be prepared for this and let it spark questions and discussion.

This group is more likely to already have some form of personal information repository already, even if that only consists of a folder full of unlabeled PDF articles. Faculty learning Zotero nearly always ask one of two questions: First, whether they can convert an existing bibliography (from a Word document, say) into Zotero citations, and second (if there are EndNote or RefWorks users in the group) whether they can convert it from one program to the other. The short answers respectively are "No, but it's usually easy to re-capture the citations from databases" and "Yes, except for the attachments."

Faculty researchers may also be citing a wider variety of sources than your average student group, so be prepared for questions about how to cite book chapters, interviews, manuscripts, legal cases or other non-book, non-article sources. As always, the more you know about your learners' information needs ahead of time, the better.

Zotero Learners: Nathan's Colleagues, Librarians

Nathan is planning Zotero training for his librarian and staff colleagues. In addition to installation and the save/cite basics, he includes:

- Common installation problems
- Synchronization and group libraries
- Frequently asked questions that may come up at the reference desk
- Best practices for teaching Zotero in workshops and IL class sessions

---

With a group of librarians, you can feel free to use a bit of jargon if it saves explanation time—at least to the extent of using the words "metadata" and "catalog record." Librarians are more likely to be involved in providing help and supporting Zotero at their institutions, so in addition to how to use it themselves, they're probably interested in common support questions. Some of these will come up in class naturally, but as you demonstrate each feature, discuss any common problems that students may have.

Expect the same wide range of comfort with technology as you would from any other class. Don't stereotype and assume that the more senior faculty members are the less tech-savvy ones in the group, but do keep an eye on the comfort level of the group and remain flexible enough to adjust the pace of the workshop as needed. If some learners are struggling with saving and editing citations, you may need to skip more advanced features planned for later in the class.

Teaching Zotero Online

As distance education becomes more common, and as students expect more and more information available remotely, it makes sense to discuss how to approach teaching Zotero online. Many libraries offer online workshops via conferencing software. Even if your library isn't doing this yet, consider investing a little time in making some brief tutorial videos as an easy way for your users to see Zotero in action.

Synchronous Classes

Synchronous online classes include anything taught live in real time, using conferencing software like Elluminate or Wimba. These programs generally allow voice chat, text chat, and screen sharing—that is, the instructor can display her own screen to the students as she teaches. This method can be a great way to teach software like Zotero, but comes with its own set of challenges.

More experienced teachers have written entire books about best practices for online teaching in general. This section just hits the highlights of some things to consider based on my experience with online Zotero classes in particular.

Attendee email

This is an email I sent to attendees of an online Zotero workshop containing all the information they needed to set up and participate. This workshop was pre-Standalone Zotero, so I stressed the need for Firefox.

Hi, everyone. You're receiving this because you've signed up for the online Zotero workshop on [date] from 10–11 a.m.

This is (as I hope you already know!) an online workshop hosted on GSU's vClass system. You'll need speakers or headphones and a broadband connection. You will be able to access the online classroom starting at 9:30 at the following link: [URL]

I'll try to start promptly at 10, so you may want to connect a couple of minutes early.

You may attend and learn without installing any additional software; just plug in your headphones and click that link above. However, you may—optionally—want to install Zotero beforehand so you can try it hands-on as we go. If so, make sure you have installed:

Firefox (http://www.mozilla.com/en-US/firefox/personal.html)— At this time Zotero requires Firefox to work. It won't work with Internet Explorer or any other web browser.

Zotero (http://www.zotero.org/)

And the Zotero/Word plugin (http://www.zotero.org/support/ word_processor_plugin_installation)

I've got instructions and more information on my Zotero web guide at http://research.library.gsu.edu/zotero.

I've had an overwhelming response for this session, and I'm excited that you're all interested in learning about Zotero! It's a great program and I think you'll find it really useful. Let me know if you have any questions and I'm looking forward to talking to you all next week.

Best, Jason

Online workshops are often more convenient for students: they can attend from home or office with no need to actually come to campus. Geographically distant students can attend, obviously, but so can your peers from other institutions. (Every online Zotero session I offer attracts at least one librarian from out of state; I am always pleased to agree to their requests to sit in.) Like a "bring your own laptop" class, they have the advantage of using a familiar computer, and after the workshop they have Zotero set up and ready to use. They need not worry about exporting or syncing any useful citations they saved during class, since they saved the items to their own computer. Synchronous online workshops also allow students to see the teaching screen up close and full size. In most cases they can use alt-Tab (or command-Tab) to switch between your presentation and their own Zotero screen to compare as the instructor demonstrates.

I usually require advance signup for online Zotero workshops. It allows me to send participants basic instructions to install Zotero on their computer beforehand. In some conference software, restarting the browser may drop students out of the session, so installing the Firefox plugin version of Zotero during class may not be practical. Instructing students to install it before class saves time and obviates restarting the browser during class. This requires that you advertise the workshop with enough lead time for you to help with installation by email if needed. (Another option is to plan the workshop as a non-interactive demonstration in which students just observe the instructor using Zotero, but of course this is less interesting for students and lacks a hands-on learning component to help reinforce the instruction.)

Advance registration also allows me to send all participants a link to log into the session, which I usually do a few days in advance. If students need to install any software other than Zotero in order to use your conferencing system, make sure to alert students to this requirement. Don't forget to mention that they need headphones to listen or a headset with microphone to participate by voice.

Teaching online carries its own pitfalls, of course. While many students (and teachers) find it convenient, it doesn't appeal to learners uncomfortable with technology. Students must install Zotero on their own, and possibly also Firefox and conference software. None of these may seem very challenging, but can seem intimidating to a technophobe or computer novice. In some areas you may need to consider whether all of your potential students have broadband internet.

Perhaps the greatest challenge to the online instructor is the fact that you can't see students' screens. Pausing to troubleshoot Zotero problems in a face-to-face class is (relatively) easy: walk over to the student's computer, see if you can spot the difficulty, and if so fix it and move on with class. In an online class, the instructor has to rely on students' verbal description of the problem to even begin to fix it. This can really bog down the class, especially if your time is limited. Solve those problems you can handle comfortably, and be prepared to follow up by email or in person for those you can't help with during class.

Consider whether you want students to ask questions via the conference software's text chat or offer the option of voice participation. Voice conferencing can make the class feel more immediate and in-person, but not all students have headsets with microphones. (A laptop's built-in mic and speakers are not usually a good substitute.) A model that works well for me is encouraging students to type discussion and questions into the text chat throughout class while I talk. It doesn't disrupt my lecture and demonstration, allows them to engage with each other as well as with me, and I pause periodically to scroll back through the chat window and make sure I haven't missed any questions. Not all instructors are comfortable with this system, so find what works best for you.

At any rate, do plan to check in regularly with students and prompt questions and comments. You have no eye contact or body language to alert you to confused or bored students, so encourage discussion and questions more actively than usual. Until you adapt to online teaching, the silent invisible audience can be slightly disconcerting.

Finally, online workshops require a more thorough pre-class technology check. Most conferencing software is fairly easy to use, but make sure you're comfortable with the screen sharing feature, the text chat, and the audio chat. Don't wait until the day of class: practice a day or more beforehand, using the actual computer and headset you will be using to teach. Don't panic when unexpected situations arise: most of your students probably have the same level of experience with online classes that you do and are likely to be forgiving when glitches happen.

Video Tutorials

Whether or not you have the ability to teach synchronous online classes, consider adding some video tutorials to your online support materials. Video demonstrations give students the opportunity to see a procedure from start to finish, with explanation, on their own screen, and the ability to pause and re-view confusing steps can be very helpful. Students can access videos for point-of-need spot instruction when workshops and technical support are unavailable.

Many programs are available for creating instructional videos: I prefer Camtasia (techsmith.com/camtasia) and its free counterpart Jing (techsmith.com/jing), but any screencasting software can work. Ideally, choose a program that allows voice narration, text labeling or subtitles, and the ability to produce a format that you can upload to YouTube. Placing your tutorials on YouTube makes them easy to embed on other sites (including your own) and makes them easy for Zotero users to find.

Make tutorials short—no more than three or four minutes long. Several short videos are preferable to one long one. Users don't usually want a start-to-finish instruction session when they look for video help; they want an explanation of the process that has them stuck at the moment. Video content isn't searchable like text, so providing a short video that gets straight to the point is the most helpful solution. Prioritize your video production in terms of the most crucial areas where your users need help, not necessarily in the same order you might teach in a class.

Supplement your self-produced tutorials with those created and shared by other Zotero experts. CHNM has produced some good examples at zotero.org/support/screencast_tutorials; these thoroughly cover all the basic save and cite features. The production values are excellent, and of course (coming straight from the source) the information is authoritative. Unfortunately at this writing CHNM has not produced any videos covering more recent features such as syncing and group libraries; hopefully that will change by the time you read this. The official CHNM videos also can't be embedded into other sites, YouTube-style; linking to them will take users off your site and onto Zotero.org, which you may or may not want.

Librarians Eric Sizemore and Jenny Veile produced an excellent example of a live Zotero demo.[8] Instructors using what I call the "five-minute demo" in class should watch this (Eric manages it in less than two). This video not only presents a quick overview of Zotero's basic features, but also shows Sizemore's potential students who he is and how he and the library can help. The simple editing between the live class and screencast feels natural and makes the video look professional, but is relatively easy to do. Sizemore and Veile take advantage of the video medium to add subtitles with links to essential resources as Sizemore teaches; viewers can pause the video at any point to get the URLs for more information.

Another good example, in a different style, is the video "Undergrads Should Love Zotero" by grad student and English composition

---

The New Orleans Research Collaborative

The New Orleans Research Collaborative (nolaresearch.org) is the most extensive teaching and research project I'm aware of that involves Zotero. This collaborative research project brings together work by undergrads, graduate students and faculty researchers to compile bibliographies on many facets of New Orleans' history and culture: labor, music, race, and the impact of Hurricane Katrina.

Research is conducted by undergraduate classes at Emory University and the University of New Orleans, with other institutions expected to participate in the near future. Students compile references in shared Zotero libraries under the guidance of faculty members. Their work is vetted by the project's editors, converted to formatted bibliographies and put on the website for other scholars' use. Because the bibliographies are COinS-enabled, any Zotero user can capture citations from the site.

At present bibliographies are created from Zotero via copy and paste, but future plans include automating the process more by converting the site to Omeka and using the Zotero-Omeka bridge for publishing.

---

instructor Rebecca (no last name or institution given, unfortunately). In this video Rebecca uses screencasts to illustrate the value of Zotero for undergraduate researchers. She accomplishes this not just with a demonstration but with entertaining discussions of the value of the personal library ("If you're selling your books back, you're going to need *something* to remind you of what you've learned"), the importance of proper citation ("Reusing text is cheating / Reusing sources is efficient") and the efficiency of Zotero as a tool ("Typing up reference lists is so 2006"). She concludes the introductory video with a suggestion to check out her other tutorial videos for more detailed instructions.[9]

Video tutorials are also a great way to illustrate specialized or novel uses for Zotero that may not be covered in the usual workshops or instructional materials. LIS lecturer and frequent presenter Kathryn Greenhill discovered that Zotero works well with Flickr to create presentation slides containing credits for the Creative Commons-licensed images she often uses. She created a short screencast of the process—certainly in less time than it would take to type up the steps and include screenshots. Because she posted the video to YouTube she was easily able to embed it into a blog post, and conference presenters searching for "Flickr and PowerPoint" tips may even be likely to discover Zotero as a result.[10]

Notes

1. CHNM's Zotero documentation includes some good examples: Center for History and New Media, "use_cases [Zotero Documentation]."

2. Deitering, "ENG 200: Library Skills for Literary Study | Get Help with a Class."; Deitering, "Zotero group bibliography assignment."; Deitering, "Zotero assignment update."; Deitering, "Zotero assignment revisions."

3. For a great example of this kind of demo, see Sizemore and Veile, *Make a Bibliography the Easy Way! Zotero Tutorial.*

4. Yorke-Barber, Ghiculescu, and Possin, "RefWorks in Three Steps."

5. Kessler and Van Ullen, "Citation Generators," 315.

6. Ibid., 316.

7. University of Michigan Institute of Museum and Library Studies, "Instructor FAQ."

8. Sizemore and Veile, *Make a Bibliography the Easy Way! Zotero Tutorial.*

9. RebeccaO321, *Undergrads Should Love Zotero.*

10. Greenhill, "Zotero and saving Flickr images. Wowza!"

Further Reading

Center for History and New Media. "screencast_tutorials [Zotero Documentation]." *Zotero*, 2010. http://www.zotero.org/support/screencast_tutorials.

———. "use_cases [Zotero Documentation]." *Zotero*, 2010. http://www.zotero.org/support/use_cases.

Croxall, Brian. "Annotated Zotero Group Bibliography Assignment", January 14, 2010. http://www.briancroxall.net/2010/01/14/annotated-zotero-group-bibliography-assignment/.

Deitering, Anne-Marie. "ENG 200: Library Skills for Literary Study | Get Help with a Class", 2011. http://ica.library.oregonstate.edu/course-guide/2761-ENG200?tab=514746.

———. "Zotero assignment revisions." *info-fetishist*, December 16, 2010. http://info-fetishist.org/2010/12/16/zotero-assignment-revisions/.

———. "Zotero assignment update." *info-fetishist*, November 8, 2010. http://info-fetishist.org/2010/11/08/zotero-assignment-update/.

———. "Zotero group bibliography assignment." *info-fetishist*, October 19, 2010. http://info-fetishist.org/2010/10/19/zotero-group-bibliography-assignment/.

Greenhill, Kathryn. *Using Zotero with Flickr Images and PowerPoint*, 2009. http://www.youtube.com/watch?v=Pr8PYdl3hR0.

———. "Zotero and saving Flickr images. Wowza!" *Librarians Matter*, September 15, 2009. http://librariansmatter.com/blog/2009/09/15/zotero-and-saving-flickr-images-wowza.

Harrison, Mary, Stephanie Summerton, and Karen Peters. "Endnote Training for Academic Staff and Students: The Experience of the Manchester Metropolitan University Library." *New Review of Academic Librarianship* 11, no. 1 (April 2005): 31–40.

Kessler, Jane, and Mary K. Van Ullen. "Citation Generators: Generating Bibliographies for the Next Generation." *Journal of Academic Librarianship* 31, no. 4 (July 1, 2005): 310–316.

McGrath, A. "RefWorks investigated: an appropriate bibliographic management solution for health students at King's College London?" *Library and Information Research News* 94 (2006): 66–73.

RebeccaO321. *Undergrads Should Love Zotero*, 2010. http://www.youtube.com/watch?v=dDoO_JxQAko.

Sample, Mark. "Sharing Research and Building Knowledge through Zotero." *Learning Through Digital Media*, February 28, 2011. http://learningthroughdigitalmedia.net/sharing-research-and-building-knowledge-through-zotero.

Sizemore, Eric, and Jenny Veile. *Make a Bibliography the Easy Way! Zotero Tutorial*, 2009. http://www.youtube.com/watch?v=Z_OUM-bZrMw.

University of Michigan Institute of Museum and Library Studies. "Instructor FAQ." *BiblioBouts*, 2011. http://bibliobouts.si.umich.edu/instructorFAQ.html.

Yorke-Barber, Phil, Cristina Ghiculescu, and Gisela Possin. "RefWorks in Three Steps: Undergraduate Team Bibliographies." *Issues in Science and Technology Librarianship*, no. 58 (January 1, 2009). http://www.istl.org/09-summer/article4.html.

Appendix A. Sample Zotero Workshop Handout (page 1)

Georgia State University Library
Jason Puckett / jpuckett@gsu.edu / IM: LibrarianJason
http://research.library.gsu.edu/zotero

What's Zotero?

Zotero [zoh-TAIR-oh] is a free, easy-to-use Firefox extension to help you collect, manage, and cite your research sources. It lives right where you do your work — in the web browser itself.

Installing Zotero

Download the Firefox plug-in

It's easy and free: Open Firefox, go to **zotero.org**, and click the big red "Download" button. Click the "Allow" button in the top right, then "Install Now" and restart Firefox when prompted.

Add Zotero to Word

Go to **http://www.zotero.org/support/microsoft_word_integration** and follow the instructions to install the Mac or Windows plugin. This will add a Zotero toolbar to MS Word. (See "Writing with Zotero and Word" below.)

The Zotero Pane

In the bottom right corner of your Firefox window you'll see a Zotero button. Click it to view or hide your "library" of saved citations. Zotero continues to run whether or not you are viewing your library.

Appendix A. Sample Zotero Workshop Handout (page 2)

Saving Citations

Zotero "watches" the pages you view to see if any of them contain citations to books, articles or other sources.

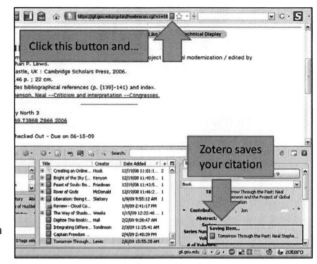

If Zotero detects that you're looking at a book or article on a catalog, database, or a site like Amazon.com, LibraryThing or the *New York Times*, you'll see a book or page icon appear in the address bar of your browser. Just click the icon and Zotero will automatically save the citation.

Saving multiple citations at once

If you're on a page of search results with many items, you'll see a folder icon instead.

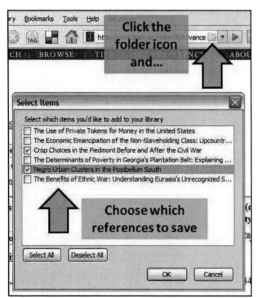

Click this to get a list of all the items on the page, and check off the ones you want to save.

Appendix A. Sample Zotero Workshop Handout (page 3)

Citing other web pages

Zotero can't automatically capture citation info from regular web pages, but you can still add them to your Zotero library.

To save a citation to a web page:

- Open your library by clicking the Zotero button

- Click the "Create new item" button to save the citation.

Zotero automatically attaches a "snapshot" of the page to the citation.

A snapshot is a copy of the page saved to your computer. It includes the page's text and images, so if the page is removed later, or if you're offline, you'll still be able to view your copy.

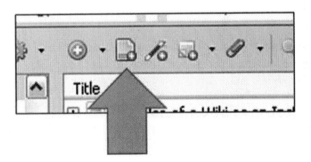

Writing with Zotero and Word

Place your cursor in your Word file exactly where you want the citation to appear. Click the ***Add-ins*** menu tab in Word 2007 to get to the Zotero toolbar. The first button on the toolbar is the Insert Citation button.

To add a citation, click the first button ("Insert Citation") on the toolbar. Select the reference you want to cite and click OK. Zotero will add the citation at your cursor.

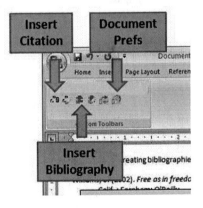

At the end of your paper, click the third button ("Insert Bibliography"). Your bibliography will appear, and new citations will be added automatically. Change bibliographic styles with the last button on the toolbar ("Set Doc Prefs").

Appendix B. Sample Zotero Online Features Handout (page 1)

Goodbye 3x5 cards.
www.zotero.org

Georgia State University Library
Jason Puckett / jpuckett@gsu.edu / IM: LibrarianJason
http://research.library.gsu.edu/zotero

Zotero: Online Features

Sync your library

zotero.org/support/sync

If you're regularly using more than one computer in your research, Zotero's sync feature can keep your library up to date on all of them. Zotero can store a copy of your library on the Zotero.org server and check it for updates whenever you open your library on a different computer. All your computers must be running the same version Zotero and be configured to sync to the server.

First, set up a (free, of course) Zotero.org user account at zotero.org/user/register.

Open Zotero preferences (via the gear menu) and select the Sync tab. Enter your Zotero user name and password. Check the "sync automatically" box. Zotero will upload your library to the server.

Repeat this configuration on each of your computers. Any updates you make on one of your computers will be reflected on the others. This even works to synchronize your library among Windows, Mac and Linux computers.

For more details and help troubleshooting sync problems, check zotero.org/support/sync.

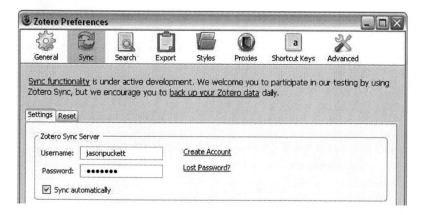

Appendix B. Sample Zotero Online Features Handout (page 2)

Zotero Groups

zotero.org/groups

Zotero's Groups feature allows you to share references with other Zotero users online. It's a great way to work on collaborative research projects.

First, set up Zotero sync as described above.

Next, log in at Zotero.org. There's a "Log In" link in the top right corner of the page.

You can search for existing public groups or create a new group at zotero.org/groups. Groups may be public (searchable, and anyone can join) or private (users can only join if invited).

You'll now have two sections in your Zotero collections pane: My Library and Group Libraries. You can drag items back and forth between them at will.

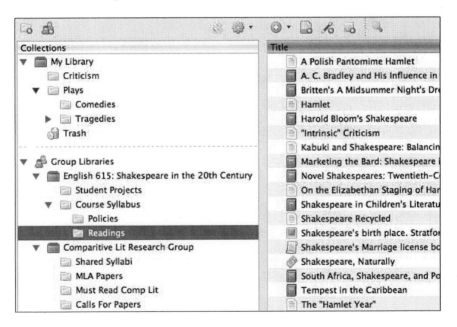

CHAPTER 7 **Supporting Zotero**

Aside from scheduled classroom learning opportunities, Zotero users often need shorter, less formal help. This may consist of a brief one-on-one consultation to help with installation, questions at the reference desk about how to use the software, technical troubleshooting, or help figuring out how to make the best use of Zotero with a particular research project.

Some of this support role may fall to the campus IT staff, but in most cases it rests within the library's portfolio. Most institutions that support Zotero have one or more librarians or reference staff who serve as the point person for Zotero teaching and help. This chapter will suggest ways to develop this Zotero "champion," move toward adopting Zotero on your campus, help other librarians and staff learn what they need to know about Zotero, and provide resources for your users to get the help they need.

The Role of the Library

Why is it up to the library to support Zotero? It's a piece of software, like Photoshop or Word or Chrome. Shouldn't the IT department be responsible for answering questions about how to use it?

This is a loaded question, but one that may come up as your institution begins to support Zotero. In fact it's a good idea to collaborate with your IT staff as you plan to adopt *any* new software, since they will probably be deeply involved in installation, upgrades and troubleshooting. Realistically, though, Zotero is a tool for researchers, no less so than a database or a catalog, and at most libraries this sort of tool is the responsibility of reference librarians to support. Your library probably has some analogous technology tools already, like GIS software or data analysis tools in which subject librarians have expertise. IT staff likely become involved in deploying Zotero to public and staff workstations, and later I'll discuss a few thoughts about best practices for collaborating with them.

This support role is a reasonable progression from the kinds of research tools librarians already support. Zotero works so closely with online search resources that showing a student how to search a database, locate and read a citation can lead quite naturally into teaching him how to save and cite that source in his own paper. In fact students often come to the reference desk for citation help already, so expecting help with citation software as well as style manuals makes sense.

Providing Zotero support offers libraries an opportunity to diversify their services and educate their users in new information tools. Librarians have found that supporting reference management software has resulted in increasing users' familiarity with other research tools,[1] increasing awareness of other instructional services offered by the libraries,[2] and in general improving visibility of library services on campus.[3]

Investing Resources

In chapter 1, I mentioned two of the uses of the word "free" that apply to open-source software like Zotero: free as in beer (available at no cost) and free as in speech (at liberty to use as you wish). A third phrase sometimes comes up in the context of supporting open-source tools: "free as in kittens." Like a kitten (usually), Zotero costs no money to acquire. Also like a kitten (always), supporting Zotero does carry long-term costs, usually in terms of staff time and effort. (Thankfully, it requires no vaccinations.)

As with any planned new service, give some thought to the resources necessary to implement Zotero support. Offering Zotero to library users is just like offering any new database in the sense that someone must be prepared to answer questions and tackle problems. Some support aspects to consider include:

Get a commitment from stakeholders in the library. This list probably includes management (such as the head of reference, instruction and/or public services), the information technology department (who will at least need to install and update the software), and service desk staff (so they can answer or refer questions appropriately). Be prepared to answer basic questions about why your library should try offering support for Zotero, either as an alternative to your existing reference manager software or as an entirely new kind of tool. Some of the points in chapter 1 may be useful to make your case (and "free" is always a big selling point).

Delineate responsibilities for supporting Zotero. Does the library have, or need, a designated Zotero "champion" or is everyone expected to have some expertise? Is Zotero expertise now part of someone's job description, and if so, do other responsibilities need to shift? If an academic department or class requests Zotero instruction, who is responsible for providing it, the Zotero trainer or the subject librarian? To what extent are reference or IT staff expected to provide Zotero help to users? (There's more about these questions in the sections Advocating for Zotero and Training Support Staff below.)

How much, and what kinds of, Zotero training can you offer your users and staff? In-person workshops, Zotero content in regular instruction sessions, one-on-one consultations, online tutorials, synchronous online classes? How will you advertise workshops? What priority do Zotero workshops receive during the busy instruction season in the first half of the semester, especially if your teaching spaces are limited?

Do you need to create a Zotero guide on your library's website? Who is responsible for updating it and how often should it be reviewed for currency? Whose contact information is listed for help?

Don't be intimidated by this list. These are probably all questions that will need consideration over time, but it's easy to start small and simply as you feel out what resources your library needs to add to your Zotero support plan. None of these items need necessarily be difficult, and not all need to be addressed before offering Zotero support. Some can be worked out over the long term.

I started out by simply asking my manager for approval to offer a Zotero workshop as an experiment to see if there was interest. Since we already offered a regularly changing roster of workshops, creating a new one was a non-issue. I installed it myself in one classroom, with the go-ahead from the IT department, and created a basic Zotero guide on the library's site at about the same time. Over time, this grew into regularly offered (and now regularly demanded) workshops and a gradually much more extensive guide, with additions and updates as I got a feel for the most common questions.[4] Our IT department head later agreed to add Zotero to the public and classroom computers as part of a regular software update between semesters.

The Zotero "Champion"

Many institutions have a Zotero "champion"—a point person for Zotero information whose responsibilities include keeping up with features, offering training (to librarians and staff and probably to library users as well), creating documentation and generally staying on top of outreach and promotion of Zotero-related services. This often includes end-user support and consultations, workshops and maintaining online guides. ("Champion" is of course used here in the sense of "supporter" or "evangelist"—not the winner of a Zotero competition....)

Many academic libraries use a subject-liaison model in which specialists with subject knowledge receive reference referrals from researchers who need their expertise. The idea of a Zotero champion fits naturally into this structure: complicated history questions go to the history librarian, business referrals to the business specialist, and Zotero questions to the Zotero specialist. It's unlikely to be someone's entire job to provide Zotero support: more likely a librarian or reference staff member becomes interested in using and teaching Zotero and offers to schedule workshops and field questions from users. This person should simply be a capable instructor, have reasonable technology competencies, and have the time and enthusiasm to take on an additional work responsibility.[5] (Taking on this role can be a potential opportunity for a library staffer who wishes to stretch her wings and get some teaching or public service experience, but who lacks subject expertise necessary to move into a liaison position.)

One benefit of having a Zotero champion in the library is that all Zotero users, within the library and in the institution as a whole, know who to approach with questions. Graduate students and faculty members in particular often learn of the Zotero specialist by word of mouth, and just as chemistry researchers can contact the chemistry librarian for research help, Zotero users will be pleased to have someone to contact for the help they need. Librarians and reference staff are usually happy to be able to refer questions rather than simply answer "I don't know" when faced with Zotero questions at the reference desk, and often incidentally learn some skills by observing the Zotero champion at work helping library users.

This model carries some downsides as well. Everyone who works in a library has experienced the case in which the needed subject specialist is out sick or on vacation, and this is no less frustrating for users or staff who need a referral to the Zotero specialist. If one person is the designated expert, it may give staff the sense that no one else needs to learn the software, which can lead to frustrating situations when the expert is unavailable. Also, if Zotero catches on in a big way at a large institution, providing support can begin to have an impact on other job duties. During the first half of the semester when demand for instruction is at its peak, a subject librarian who is also the library's Zotero champion may find his time at a premium. (On the other hand, many requests for Zotero help take place later in the semester, during the writing phase rather than the early research phase.)

The Zotero champion can take steps to help counteract these potential problems. First, offer brief refresher training sessions for public services staff. A good time for this may be during breaks when students and faculty are off campus and library staff often have some unscheduled time. Ideally, librarians and management regard reference manager software as an information resource along the lines of other tools like databases, and can help encourage everyone who works public service desks to acquire enough competency with it to handle basic questions. Schedule Zotero workshops for the public around the anticipated class instruction peaks in the semester, either during the first week or two before library instruction gets busy, or after midterms when it tends to taper off. Provide good online documentation on the library website so that both staff and users have help to refer to in the absence of the Zotero expert.

The new Zotero champion should remember that she's not alone—Zotero has an active support community to share problems, help and suggestions. Use the forums on the Zotero website (forums.zotero.org) and the Zotero Evangelists listserv (groups.google.com/group/zotero-evangelists) for advice.

Collaborating with Administration and IT

Make sure you have support from someone in your library's management; whether this is your immediate department head or someone higher up will depend on your situation, of course. It's probably a good idea in any case to clear it with the appropriate reference or instruction manager before offering a new service like Zotero support, and they can support you in discussions with administrators if there's need. The Educause document "7 Things You Should Know About Zotero" is a good non-technical overview if you need a clear introduction to Zotero.[6]

The "free" factor can be a valuable argument, especially if you are considering it as an option that could replace a costly commercial product down the line.

Your IT department will be also important collaborators as you adopt Zotero at your institution. They will most likely be the ones installing it, rolling it out to your public computers (and possibly staff computers as well), and managing updates. You'll almost certainly need them to buy into your plans for Zotero to some degree. Since offering a new piece of software on the library computers requires a commitment on their part, you may need to make the case for Zotero.

Be willing to start small; even if you want to install Zotero on all of your public computers, your technology staff may want to evaluate it on a smaller scale. Consider installing it in one of your instruction rooms to use as a Zotero lab for training. Failing that, request sufficient administrator rights to install it on classroom computers yourself before teaching and offer to manage its technical support yourself. This is usually a very low-maintenance responsibility. The Firefox plugin can often be installed on computers even without admin rights, so you may already have the access you need. (Do get appropriate approvals before proceeding, though, even if you can get the technology working on your own.)

If you can get Zotero set up on a small scale, give the experiment time to work for a while—perhaps a semester or so—before pushing for expansion. Teach some workshops for faculty and students, give some basic training to librarians and staff, and make sure that you're having no technical difficulties. Some librarians have reported to me that once Zotero got a toehold on campus, their faculty began to specifically request it, which led naturally to setting it up on public computers.

Don't worry. You probably won't need all this advice, but it may help if you need to persuade anyone in your organization as you plan to adopt Zotero.

Campus Outreach

Library users can now get much of their research material online without visiting the library, and so don't always appreciate the library's role in the process. Zotero can provide an excellent opportunity for outreach and to promote library services. Audiences to consider when planning Zotero outreach include.[7]

The library: some of the most appreciative audiences for Zotero outreach consist of library colleagues. Reference and instruction librarians and staff benefit from training and information about Zotero's features to assist users, and subject librarians often help promote the software to their departments. Library colleagues can also suggest other avenues for promotion and outreach.

Faculty: subject liaison librarians in particular have plenty of opportunities for faculty outreach. Zotero outreach and presentations can take place at campus-wide technology events, brown-bag learning sessions, and other professional development opportunities. As the people who most influence your students' academic careers, faculty members can in turn recommend and promote Zotero to students.

Students: Student organizations can be effective in creating peer evangelists. Aside from formally scheduled workshops and class sessions, Zotero can be of interest to other student departments and programs on campus. Writing centers, peer tutoring programs and academic honor societies are good audiences for Zotero information. If your campus has an open-source or free culture advocacy group (like a Linux users' group, Students for Free Culture, or similar organizations), Zotero can be an interesting and useful way for them to apply their extracurricular interests to a practical research tool.

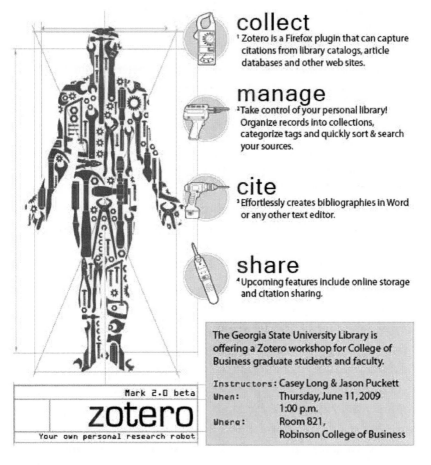

what is zotero?

A free program for saving citations & creating bibliographies. An all-purpose research power tool.

collect
[1] Zotero is a Firefox plugin that can capture citations from library catalogs, article databases and other web sites.

manage
[2] Take control of your personal library! Organize records into collections, categorize tags and quickly sort & search your sources.

cite
[3] Effortlessly creates bibliographies in Word or any other text editor.

share
[4] Upcoming features include online storage and citation sharing.

The Georgia State University Library is offering a Zotero workshop for College of Business graduate students and faculty.

Instructors: Casey Long & Jason Puckett
When: Thursday, June 11, 2009
               1:00 p.m.
Where: Room 821,
               Robinson College of Business

Mark 2.0 beta

zotero

Your own personal research robot

Figure 7.1. Figure: Flyer for a Zotero workshop by GSU Library Creative Manager Christian Steinmetz. Christian chose a footnote/citation motif for several of our Zotero promotions to suggest at a glance that this is a citation tool.

Promotional Materials

Make sure your users have the opportunity to hear about your Zotero services and events by giving them publicity on your website and in public spaces.

If your library has a blog, you already probably use that space for announcing new events, resources and services; include info about your Zotero workshops and any significant new features. This can be a good way to position the library as a resource for new cutting-edge research technologies. In terms of real spaces, create paper flyers to post in the library, but get permission to post in appropriate departmental spaces where students and faculty will encounter them. The reference desk may be a good place to offer paper handouts as well.

SAVE TIME CREATING BIBLIOGRAPHIES
SIGN UP FOR A LIBRARY WORKSHOP

zotero   [1] jpuckett@gsu.edu,
Zotero Workshop.
Library North, Classroom 1,
10:00 a.m., 13 September 2010

Figure 7.2. Website ad for a Zotero workshop by GSU Library Creative Manager Christian Steinmetz. This banner ad rotates on the home page of the library site for about two weeks before the class takes place.

what is zotero?

Georgia State University Library provides access to and instruction on two programs designed to save citations & create bibliographies. Endnote is free software for GSU students, faculty and staff. Zotero is an add-on for the Mozilla Firefox browser and is free to download for anyone. Collect, manage, cite & share your citations all in one place!

Figure 7.3. Website ad promoting Zotero as a library service. This image rotates on the library's home page year-round in addition to ads promoting other services.

Graphics can attract attention to a post or flyer. If you have a talented graphic designer on staff, see if you can impose on their time to design website ads or paper flyers. If not, the Center for History and New Media has given permission to use any text and images from the Zotero website for support and promotional materials.[8]

Don't assume that your readers know what Zotero is or does. Make sure your posts and flyers include a prominent line or two about what Zotero is and does in addition to the times, dates and locations of your workshops.

Online Guides

Your library should provide some form of online guide for Zotero users. This guide serves several functions. Of course, first and foremost it provides instructions and information so users can get help when the Zotero experts are unavailable. It can also provide a "landing point" where your users can discover Zotero's existence, and discover that the library offers Zotero training and support services. Finally, like any research guide in the library, it can serve as a jumping-off point for more information and related resources.

Librarians often have a tendency to provide too much explanatory text on research guides. Bear in mind that for web readers, less is often more. Short bullet point lists of instructions catch the eye better than a long paragraph of text. Readers may be coming to your guide for an explanation of a particular process; make sure they can spot the information they need rather than having to hunt for it.

Include screenshots. Often illustrating a process is easier than explaining it in text. Annotate images and visually highlight the feature, button, or area of the screen with the key information. (PowerPoint is a useful program for annotating screenshots. Paste in a screenshot, add arrows, circles and/or text, and save the resulting annotated slide as an image.)

Embedded videos on a guide can add commentary and "live" demonstrations of procedures. Keep them short so that users don't have to wade through a long video just to see the key step they need. Remember that search engines can't index the content of a video, so accompany them with text captions.

If your users are familiar with other reference managers like Mendeley or EndNote, and especially if Zotero is new to your institution, consider including a comparison chart to give them an idea of what each program can and can't do. If you recommend different programs for their different strengths, include notes to that effect. Readers will probably appreciate your honest recommendations.

Include information about relevant workshops and events. If you tag Zotero-related posts consistently on your library blog, you may be able to feed just those posts into your Zotero guide. (Research guide products like LibGuides provide an easy mechanism for this; otherwise, ask your web librarian.) CHNM's Zotero blog provides product news and updates.

Make sure that it is someone's responsibility—usually that of the Zotero champion—to periodically review the page and keep the information current. Guides to software tend to drop out of currency and become outdated more quickly than subject or course guides, and CHNM adds new improvements and features on a regular basis.

This sounds like a lot of work, and it can be, but the Zotero community has already created a lot of this material and makes it available to share and copy. Again, CHNM has given permission to use any images from the official Zotero site in your own documentation, and their screencast tutorials are excellent. Marie Sciangula of Purchase College SUNY has created two excellent examples: her LibGuide (purchase. libguides.com/zotero) and a training course built in Moodle (tinyurl. com/purchase-zotero; click the guest login button).[9] My own Zotero guide (research.library.gsu.edu/zotero) is published under a Creative Commons license granting permission for anyone to copy and adapt it as long as credit for the original is kept intact. For many other examples, see zotero.org/support/third_party_documentation.

Training Support Staff

If public services librarians and staff are expected to provide Zotero support, of course the library must put some effort into training them. Make sure the library provides its staff with support in the form of training sessions, online guides for later reference, and ideally teaching materials that individual instructors can adapt and improve upon for their own use.

Training sessions should cover not only how to use Zotero, but discussion of common problems, questions and answers that support staff will need to know. The most common questions about Zotero simply have to do with setting it up and using the basic save and cite features, and most librarians can pick these up quickly with a demonstration and a little hands-on experience.

Front-line support staff should be able to handle common questions such as:

- Installation, including the word processor toolbars (chapter 2)
- Importing and exporting between Zotero and any other reference manager supported by the library (chapter 3)
- Attaching PDFs to citations (chapter 3)
- Using copy/paste or the Word toolbar to create bibliographies (chapter 4)
- Exporting references from a library computer to a flash drive, or vice versa, via the right-click Export function (chapter 3)
- Any idiosyncratic problems using Zotero with popular library resources (does Zotero have trouble saving from your library catalog, for example? Does it work with your metasearch tools?)
- Setting up the basic sync function (chapter 5)
- Converting Word bibliographies into a Zotero collection (there's no simple or automatic way to do this, but the question comes up frequently)
- And more at zotero.org/support/frequently_asked_ questions and zotero.org/support/getting_help

Of course, it is still useful to have a designated expert who can handle referrals for problems and advanced questions.

Instructors who teach Zotero regularly will find it useful to share their training materials like workshop outlines, handouts, and slides with the rest of the library staff, or perhaps even on your public Zotero guide. This can encourage other busy library instructors to branch out into including Zotero in their own course-related instruction, or even offering Zotero training themselves.

New Zotero trainers can provide backup by co-teaching in classes taught by more experienced instructors. This provides benefit to the experienced trainer in the form of a teaching assistant who can circulate to provide on the spot help during hands-on activities. The new instructor benefits by learning during the class, hearing common recurring questions from students and faculty, and asking their own questions during the session. They can even trade roles as the new instructor takes over a primary role in later classes, with the more experienced Zotero trainer providing scaffolding for the first few sessions until the new instructor is comfortable teaching solo.

Notes

1. Harrison, Summerton, and Peters, "Endnote Training for Academic Staff and Students," 37.
2. Ibid., 38.
3. Siegler and Simboli, "EndNote at Lehigh."
4. Puckett, "Zotero [GSU Library guide]."
5. Harrison, Summerton, and Peters, "Endnote Training for Academic Staff and Students," 33.
6. Educause, "7 Things You Should Know About Zotero."
7. Duong, "Rolling Out Zotero Across Campus as a Part of a Science Librarian's Outreach Efforts," 321–322.
8. Center for History and New Media, "adopt [Zotero Documentation]."
9. Sciangula, "Zotero Citation Management Tool."; Sciangula, "Zotero: Scholarly Research Tool."

Further Reading

At this writing, a few articles about adopting and supporting Zotero in academic libraries are starting to appear in LIS and education journals, and I expect to see many more in the next few years. Don't overlook the work about supporting other reference managers that has been published for the last several years, however: the good advice in articles about supporting RefWorks and EndNote is easily generalizable to Zotero as well.

Center for History and New Media. "adopt [Zotero Documentation]." *Zotero*, 2010. http://www.zotero.org/support/adopt.

———. "getting_stuff_into_your_library [Zotero Documentation]." *Zotero*, 2010.

http://www.zotero.org/support/getting_stuff_into_your_library.

————. "kb:importing_records_from_endnote [Zotero Documentation]." *Zotero*, 2009. http://www.zotero.org/support/kb/importing_records_from_endnote.

————. "third_party_documentation [Zotero Documentation]." *Zotero*, 2010. http://www.zotero.org/support/third_party_documentation.

Duong, Khue. "Rolling Out Zotero Across Campus as a Part of a Science Librarian's Outreach Efforts." *Science & Technology Libraries* 29, no. 4 (2010): 315–324.

East, J. W. "Academic libraries and the provision of support for users of personal bibliographic software: a survey of Australian experience with EndNote." *LASIE* 32, no. 1 (2001): 64–70.

Educause. "7 Things You Should Know About Zotero." *Educause*, 2008. http://www.educause.edu/ELI/7ThingsYouShouldKnowAboutZoter/163217.

George Mason University Libraries. "Citation Migration", 2008. http://citationmigration.gmu.edu/.

Harrison, Mary, Stephanie Summerton, and Karen Peters. "Endnote Training for Academic Staff and Students: The Experience of the Manchester Metropolitan University Library." *New Review of Academic Librarianship* 11, no. 1 (April 2005): 31–40.

McGrath, A. "RefWorks investigated: an appropriate bibliographic management solution for health students at King's College London?" *Library and Information Research News* 94 (2006): 66–73.

Princeton University Library. "Export to RW/EN/Zotero." *Using RefWorks at Princeton*, 2011. http://libguides.princeton.edu/content.php?pid=30227&sid=230429.

Puckett, Jason. "Zotero [GSU Library guide]", 2011. http://research.library.gsu.edu/zotero.

Sciangula, Marie. "Zotero Citation Management Tool." *Purchase College Library*, 2011. http://purchase.libguides.com/zotero.

————. "Zotero: Scholarly Research Tool", n.d. http://moodle.purchase.edu/moodle/course/view.php?id=945.

Siegler, S., and B. Simboli. "EndNote at Lehigh." *Issues in Science and Technology Librarianship* 32 (2002).

About the Author

Jason Puckett is Communication Librarian at Georgia State University in Atlanta, Georgia. He was named a *Library Journal* Mover and Shaker for 2010, in part for his work with Zotero. He's the co-host and co-producer of the Adventures in Library Instruction podcast (adlibinstruction.blogspot.com) about information literacy teaching in libraries.

Puckett has a BA in English from Georgia State University and an MLIS from Florida State University, and has worked in libraries since 1993. He is a B-movie fan and an enthusiastic but unskilled video gamer. He lives online at jasonpuckett.net.

More links and information about this book are available at jasonpuckett.net/zotero. The bibliography is available as a public group library at zotero.org/groups/z_guide_by_puckett. GSU's Zotero guide, shared under a Creative Commons license, is available at research.library.gsu.edu/zotero.